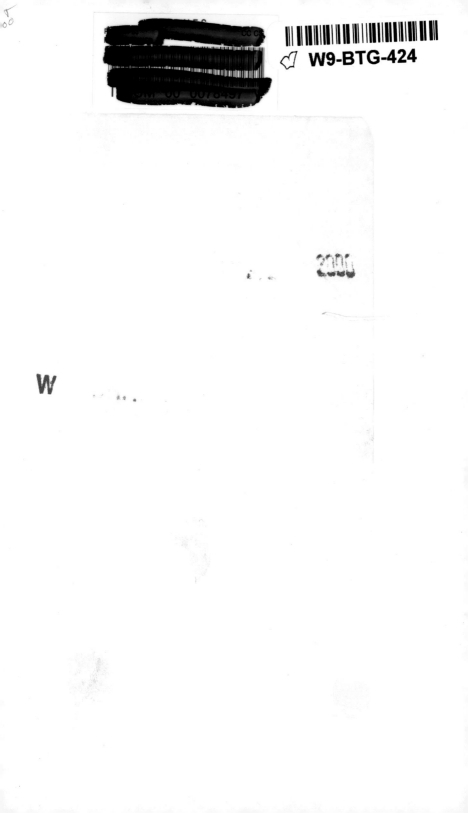

W

Essays & Studies 1982

THE POET'S POWER

Essays & Studies
1982

THE POET'S POWER

Collected by
Suheil Bushrui

HUMANITIES PRESS
Atlantic Highlands, N.J.

83-683

ESSAYS AND STUDIES 1982
IS VOLUME THIRTY-FIVE IN THE NEW SERIES
OF ESSAYS AND STUDIES COLLECTED ON BEHALF OF
THE ENGLISH ASSOCIATION

© The English Association 1982

First published 1982

Typeset by Inforum Ltd, Portsmouth
Printed by The Pitman Press

ISBN 0-391-02622-4

Foreword

To say that it is a singular honour to be asked by the English Association to follow in the footsteps of men like Geoffrey Tillotson, Geoffrey Bullough, Sir George Rostrevor Hamilton, Basil Willey, Simeon Potter and A.R. Humphreys, all past collectors of *Essays and Studies*, would be to state the obvious. And yet for such an honour to have fallen to someone other than a British subject, as Professor George Steiner remarked of his presidency of the Association in 1975, is something quite special. I am deeply grateful for this unique opportunity.

As an outsider to English Literature and a long-standing student of Arabic Literature, I naturally have preferences somewhat different from those of my predecessors as collectors. Nevertheless, the values of these two great literatures have so much in common that I could not fail to be moved by the nobility and richness of English poetry; indeed, my appreciation of it is greatly enhanced by being able to compare two quite separate poetic traditions.

The theme I have chosen for this volume is 'the Poet's Power in English Literature'. This is divided into seven ages, from Chaucer, Shakespeare, Milton and Pope through to Blake, Tennyson and Yeats. In seeking contributors to the volume I naturally approached people with similar convictions to my own, and they have responded in a manner far exceeding my hopes. Each of these essays bears the individual stamp of its author and yet the theme can be discerned throughout. Perhaps no other theme could be more relevant in these times, for who better to provide our leaders with guidance than visionary poets? Did not Shelley call them 'the unacknowledged legislators of the world'?

Suheil Bushrui
American University of Beirut
Lebanon

Beneath the throne of God lie treasures the keys to which are the tongues of poets.

(From the Sayings of the Prophet Muhammad)

In the long run, it is the great writer of a nation that becomes its image in the minds of posterity, and even though he represent no man of worth in his art, the worth of his own mind becomes the inheritance of his people. He takes nothing away that he does not give back in greater volume.

(W.B. Yeats, 'Samhain: 1905', *Explorations,* p. 192)

. . . I do believe, as you do, that the world can be saved—or that human beings can be saved from the world—only by Imagination, which . . . is the expression of our true humanity . . . But we live in a world of materialism . . . What can poetry—the language of the immortal human spirit, which Blake calls the Imagination and identifies with the Christian Logos itself . . . mean in society which denies this spirit by its very definition?. . . Thus the very name of 'Poetry' has been usurped and manipulated, and the true essential of all the arts suppressed or merely lost sight of in a welter of so-called 'self-expression' whether of the sentimental or nihilist kind.

(Kathleen Raine, from a letter to the editor of *New Departures,* 1981)

Much of his (the poet's) power comes from his being in reaction against the scientific spirit, which is the driving force of our century. Like many others, he seeks to escape from the bleak, uncomforting conclusions of science to what touches the heart, and both his visions and his methods are not so much unscientific as antiscientific.

(C.M. Bowra, *Poetry and Politics, 1900–1960,* p. 36)

Contents

I   REALMS AND APPROXIMATIONS: SOURCES OF
    CHAUCER'S POWER   1
    Robert Burchfield

II THE POET AND TABOO: THE RIDDLE OF
    SHAKESPEARE'S 'PERICLES'   14
    John Pitcher

III THE APPROPRIATION OF MILTON   30
    Bernard Sharratt

IV POPE'S WASTELAND: REFLECTIONS ON
    MOCK-HEROIC   45
    Claude Rawson

V   BLAKE: THE POET AS PROPHET   66
    Kathleen Raine

VI TENNYSON AND SOME DOUBTS   84
    Alastair Thomson

VII YEATS: THE POET AS HERO   101
    Suheil Bushrui

    Notes on contributors   124

Contents

I

Realms and Approximations: Sources of Chaucer's Power

ROBERT BURCHFIELD

I

O, a noble thyng and a cleer thyng is power that is nat fownden myghty to kepe itself! And yif that power of remes be auctor and makere of blisfulnesse, yif thilke power lakketh on any syde, amenuseth [diminishes] it nat thilke blisfulnesse and bryngeth in wrecchidnesse?[1]

Power and realms. Blissfulness and wretchedness. These are themes to which Chaucer constantly returns. In pursuit of them he ransacked the ancients, often at more than one remove. He pillaged the literary works of several countries, both of his own time and of the slightly obsolescent past. He accepted the Christian heritage of Western Europe as the main pillar of his spiritual beliefs. He mastered the rhetorical arts and systematically decorated his themes by means of them. He accepted the beliefs of his contemporaries about the nature of the universe, about the social and political arrangements of his own country—how could he do otherwise? —and about the structure and condition of the human body. He loved 'the labour of olde astrologiens':[2] astrology was verifiable, if not in his own experience at any rate in the lives of kings and heroes, real or imaginary, demonstrably changed by the influential positioning of the planets. He adored chivalry, beauty, 'layes' (of love or adventure), and ancient books. He described the tattered pockets and worn sleeves of the society of his own time as well as its noble garments. He sought out the mysteries of the past and turned them to his poetic advantage, while never losing sight of the fluctuating 'welefulness' and wretchedness of his own day: for example, we find

---

[1] Chaucer's *Boece* Bk III, Prosa 5, 7–13. The quotations are all cited from F.N. Robinson's standard (second) edition (Oxford, 1957).

[2] *Astr.* Pref. 62.

him drawing together the fear of Custance in *The Man of Law's Tale*
and that of a criminal in fourteenth-century London:

> Have ye nat seyn somtyme a pale face,
> Among a prees, of hym that hath be lad
> Toward his deeth, wher as hym gat no grace,
> And swich a colour in his face hath had,
> Men myghte knowe his face that was bistad,
> Amonges alle the faces in that route?
> So stant Custance, and looketh hire aboute.[3]

No field marshal commanded an army more skillfully than
Chaucer commanded his own language—an already motley array
of native and foreign elements, weldable in the proper hands into an
instrument of noble power.

These were his realms and limitless territories and he the matchless
monarch and emperor of them all.

II

And the bank of that river consists partly of hard rock, subject to
no alteration or only to an imperceptible one, partly of sand,
which now in one place now in another gets washed away, or
deposited.[4]

The stylistic components of twelfth- and thirteenth-century
France, the teachings of 'Olde Ypocras, Haly, and Galyen',[5] the
legends of 'Thise olde gentil Britouns in hir dayes',[6] these and many
other things were Chaucer's 'hard rock', not in their fundamentals
subject to alteration. But the poems that he wrote did not turn out to
be simple adaptations of them nor amalgams of a series of borrowed
constituent parts. No poem of Chaucer's is like an object assembled
from prefabricated components. The amalgamation is more subtle
and infinitely more elusive. Each of his realms merely approximates
to the realms he inherited. In lesser poets of his time the borrowed
elements protrude like the bones of a starving animal in a desert.
Chaucer absorbs and masters them to the point that the 'deposited
sand' is often more beautiful and more instructive than the 'hard

---

[3] *CT* B[1]. 645–51.
[4] Tr. L. Wittgenstein, *On Certainty* (Oxford, 1979 impression), proposition 99.
[5] *CT* A. Prol. 431.
[6] *CT* F. 709.

rock'. The poet beside the Thames built fabrics and designs of incomparable power and was the only poet in this country between the early eighth century and his own day who did so: others had moments of memorable power but no one else before him could sustain the grandeur for long.

III

The propositions describing this world-picture might be part of a kind of mythology. And their role is like that of rules of a game; and the game can be learned practically, without learning any explicit rules.[7]

A great poet displays the rules of his art without appearing to have learned them in any explicit way. This is true of Chaucer whether one thinks of his use of the colours of rhetoric or of the themes of which, he declares, 'olde bookes maken us memorie',[8] or of any other part of his work. Once a catalogue of his sources has been assembled—diligent scholars have seen to that—it is not profitable to wonder whether Chaucer drew on Galen or Constantinus Africanus or Gilbertus Anglicus for his knowledge of the four humours, or on some other traditional sources concerning the four elements in creation, earth, air, fire, and water. The value lies in the skill with which this ordinary knowledge is absorbed within the verse. The grief of Arcite is placed like an emotional ring round the physics of one of these concepts:

> But I, that am exiled and bareyne
> Of alle grace, and in so greet dispeir,
> That ther nys erthe, water, fir, ne eir,
> Ne creature that of hem maked is,
> That may me helpe or doon confort in this,
> Wel oughte I sterve in wanhope and distresse.
> Farwel my lif, my lust, and my gladnesse![9]

Similarly, 'faire Pertelote' gives comfort to her 'herte deere' Chauntecleer who was 'drecched soore' because of a dream (a 'sweven'):

[7] Tr. L. Wittgenstein, *On Certainty* (Oxford, 1979 impression), proposition 95.
[8] *CT* B². 3164.
[9] *CT* A. 1244–50.

Nothyng, God woot, but vanitee in sweven is.
Swevenes engendren of repleccriouns,
And ofte of fume and of complecciouns,
Whan humours been to habundant in a wight.
Certes this dreem, which ye han met to-nyght,
Cometh of the greete superfluytee
Of youre rede colera, pardee,
Which causeth folk to dreden in hir dremes
Of arwes, and of fyr with rede lemes,
Of rede beestes, that they wol hem byte,
Of contek, and of whelpes, grete and lyte.[10]

The medical details, recorded elsewhere in manuals of the same century, lie embedded here in the serio-comic dialogue of an animal world, adding subtlety to the factuality of the context and ending by being distant from, though still visibly proximate to, the source of the knowledge.

IV

I formed and executed a plan of study for the use of my Trans-alpine expedition: the typography of old Rome, the ancient geography of Italy, and the science of medals.[11]

Gibbon's life was one of indefatigable scholarship and the results are set down in *The Decline and Fall of the Roman Empire*. The scholarly realms he mastered concerned the virtues and abilities of real historical figures like Nerva, Trajan, Hadrian, and the two Antonines, civil wars, seditions, violent deaths, tyrannies, and the rise of Christianity. Chaucer like Gibbon was a European; he was endowed with a sense of history but was not a historian or even a chronicler, and certainly not an exact scholar. Gibbon, one feels, would have been regarded by Chaucer as one of

alle these clerkes
That writen of Romes myghty werkes.[12]

and gently set aside with a dismissive couplet:

[10] *CT* B².4112–22.
[11] Edward Gibbon, *Autobiography* (Oxford, World's Classics, 1907), p. 141.
[12] *HF* 1503–4.

That yf y wolde her names telle,
Al to longe most I dwelle.[13]

Historical events had no value in themselves for Chaucer except in so far as they exemplified the laws of Dame Fortune, the constancy of women in love, or any of his other recurring themes. For Edward Gibbon 'there is not any argument, any circumstance, which can melt a fable into allegory'.[14] Chaucer melted legend and myth into the reality of his own century; he also interpreted historical events as demonstrations of the perennial nature of traditional concepts.

Nevertheless there were things that Chaucer observed with minute care.

> The poet whose favourite metaphors for the making of poetry were drawn from field and barn and furrow must have watched with a special attentiveness the life of the mill.[15]

The late Professor Bennett (my former tutor) brought all his resources and experience to bear on the problem of verisimilitude in *The Miller's Tale* and *The Reeve's Tale*. Particular details, obscure or unnoticed since the Middle Ages, were clarified as he examined the rolls, receipts, and charters of medieval Oxbridge manciples and parish clerks.

> In Chaucerian studies today whoso would do any good—to apply an apophthegm of Blake's—must do it in minute particulars.[16]

The *kymelyn*,[17] a tray or trough used in college halls or kitchens, and the *jubbe*[18] procured for Nicholas, the student of *The Miller's Tale*, by his Oxford landlord, are confirmed from contemporary records.[19] The horse in *The Reeve's Tale* is called 'Bayard', a name found 'more

---

[13] *HF* 1505–6.
[14] *Autobiogr.* (World's Classics), p. 170.
[15] J.A.W. Bennett, *Chaucer at Oxford and at Cambridge* (Oxford, 1974), p. 116.
[16] Ibid., p. 2.
[17] a knedyng trogh, And after that a tubbe and a kymelyn. *CT* A. 3620–1.
[18] good ale in a jubbe. Ibid. 3628.
[19] Stephano le joignur, pro j kembelina subtus cisternam Regis, vijd.—A roll of Edward I; et pro uno pare jobbes de iiij galonibus.—Accounts for the 1392 expedition of the poet's patron, the Earl of Derby (the future Henry IV).

than once' in the fourteenth-century Rolls of Merton College, Oxford. The young men who went up to Oxford were not, as so often in later centuries, drawn from well-to-do families, but were mostly from religious houses and the poorer classes—genuinely *pauperes scholares*—the *poure scoleres* of Chaucer. When singing *Angelus ad virginem* Nicholas, in *The Miller's Tale*, was simply following 'the collegiate custom of singing the Antiphon to the Virgin after compline or the evening collation'.[20] The interior of John's house can be more or less reconstructed from details provided by Chaucer when these are set against surviving descriptions of houses of the period in Oxford,[21] gables, 'shot-wyndowe' (A.3358), bowers, and all.

Of course such small observational discoveries are welcome. Yet it would have been surprising if Chaucer had misreported things that lay under his very eyes.

When one turns away from masonry and mills, however, Chaucer is much less evidently concerned with visual confirmation of the objects all round him than with the approximations to reality which made up the normal poetical kit of a poet of the fourteenth century. This can be demonstrated in various ways. For example, at an extremely mundane level, vegetables were no more important to Chaucer than they were to other writers of the time. The Summoner

Wel loved he garleek, oynons, and eek lekes.[22]

And Antony, at war with Octavian,

He poureth pesen upon the haches slidere.[23]

But, with rare exceptions,[24] Chaucer normally refers to vegetables only in disparaging terms as symbolic emblems of worthlessness:

[20] J.A.W. Bennett, ibid., p. 31.
[21] Ibid., pp. 34 ff.
[22] *CT* A. 634.
[23] *LGW* 648.
[24] There are no examples in Chaucer's works of *chibol* (Welsh onion), *chicory*, *cole* (cabbage), *lettuce*, *neep*, *parsnip*, or *radish*, nor of the herbs *chervil*, *majoram*, *purslane*, *rue*, or *thyme*, though these words are recorded in other writers of his time or earlier. *Mint* and *fennel* occur in the same line (731) of the *Romaunt of the Rose*, and *parsley* once in *The Prologue of the Cook's Tale* (A. 4350). The names of other vegetables and herbs that are now very familiar, for example *carrot*, *chick-pea*, *potato*, *rosemary*, *spinach*, and *tomato*, did not enter the language until after Chaucer's death.

God help me so, I counte hem nought a bene![25]

Of paramours he sette nat a kers [cress].[26]

And seyden they yeven noght a lek
For fame ne for such renoun.[27]

The lack of closely observed detail is confirmed when one turns to the terms connected with ships and the sea. One of the Canterbury pilgrims is a 'shipman' and there is a shipwreck in *The Man of Law's Tale*. Chaucer himself crossed and recrossed the Channel in the 1360s and the 1370s. But the vocabulary he uses is that of a landlubber: well-known words occur, like *anchor, barge, boat, mast, oar, sail, ship*, and so on, but none of the more precise terminology known from other sources in the fourteenth century (and earlier). One looks in vain for *bowsprit, hawser, keel, larboard, luff, reef* (used by Gower), *rudder, starboard, stay, stem, stern* (used by Usk), and many others. No details distinguish the barges, boats, and ships mentioned in the poems. They often appear in conjunction in a generalized context:

Where as she many a ship and barge seigh
Seillynge hir cours.[28]

Ye remoeve alle the rokkes, stoon by stoon,
That they ne lette ship ne boot to goon.[29]

For men may overlade a ship or barge.[30]

For thogh so be that ship or boot here come.[31]

With hym com many a ship and many a barge.[32]

When a more specific type of vessel is mentioned, it appears indirectly in an intentionally unusual comparison and is seen from a distance with sails furled:

'And now hath Sathanas,' seith he, 'a tayl
Brodder than of a carryk is the sayl.'[33]

In short, Chaucer's ships are those of a child's drawing, undifferentiated representations of the notion 'ship', just vessels that go to sea.

[25] *TC* V. 363.   [26] *CT* A. 3756.   [27] *HF* 1708–9.
[28] *CT* F. 850–1.   [29] Ibid. 993–4.   [30] *LGW* 621.
[31] Ibid. 2215.   [32] Ibid. 2407.   [33] *CT* D. 1687–8.

V

Our worlds wax and wane with a difference. We belong to different tribes.[34]

Chaucer's world was not ours, nor in most respects was his tribe the same as ours. The passage of the centuries carries along with it only part of the systems and beliefs of the past. The remainder is left behind as disassembled rubble, not rebuildable even by skilled hands. To revisit the poems of Chaucer, as I have done in order to write this essay, is to go back, as it were, to one's old haunts, etched at the time so clearly in one's mind, but, when revisited, found to be covered over by new buildings, somewhat strange, not as one remembered them.

Professor Bushrui asked me to write an essay 'for the sake of the Third World', a concept undreamt of in the fourteenth century. The Middle Eastern part of the Third World was for Chaucer a poetical rather than a geographical entity. *Achemenie* (in Persia), *Palatye* (in Anatolia), and *Satalye* (in Turkey) are placed before our eyes as satisfactory reminders of a generalized heathendom or 'Barbarie'. The 'Barbre nacioun' Syria is the setting for the *prima pars* of *The Man of Law's Tale*, and there is also a passing reference to Syria when 'Ne Surrien, ne noon Arabyen'[35] dared engage in battle with 'Cenobia, of Palymerie queene'. The Persians who, Chaucer says, have written about her are ghostly and anonymous. Custance, 'in a ship al steereless', glides over 'the salte see'

> Thurghout the See of Grece unto the Strayte
> Of Marrok.[36]

The Knight had fought in the Middle East:

> At Alisaundre he was whan it was wonne.

But the names of the other battlefields resound like the noise of distant bells:

> In Lettow hadde he reysed and in Ruce,
> No Cristen man so ofte of his degree.
> In Gernade at the seege eek hadde he be
> Of Algezir, and ridden in Belmarye . . .

[34] Iris Murdoch, *Nuns and Soldiers* (London, 1980), p. 5.
[35] *CT* B². 3529.   [36] *CT* B¹. 464–5.

They seem (and were meant to sound) romantically distant and remote, as unimaginably removed from the banks of the Thames as 'the soleyn fenix of Arabye'[37] or the 'Affrike of the worthy Cipioun'.[38]

Cyprus is just glanced at by Chaucer as the Monk presents his cameo portraits under the heading *De Casibus Virorum Illustrium*. After Hercules

> Thus starf this worthy, myghty Hercules.
> Lo, who may truste on Fortune any throwe?[39]

Balthasar

> He was out cast of mannes compaignye;
> With asses was his habitacioun.[40]

and Cenobia

> Allas, Fortune! she that whilom was
> Dredeful to kynges and to emperoures,
> Now gaureth al the peple on hire, allas![41]

comes 'worthy Petro, kyng of Cipre', slain in his bed 'for no thyng but for chivalrie'.[42] Yet it was in Cyprus last year that I found a vantage-point from which I could see, or thought I could see, the world in which Chaucer moved with something of the clarity of a medieval 'sweven'. Deep down in a valley, the rocky slopes of which were covered with carobs and olive-trees, pines, cypresses, and sweet-scented herbs, about six miles north-west of Ktima, is the retreat of a Byzantine saint, St Neophytos. Secluded, close to the immutabilities of Nature, a place once sought out by pilgrims, a seat of learning, and yet originally just a set of caves, it seemed to represent the essence of one of Chaucer's realms. The caves were like the one inhabited by Morpheus and Eclympasteyr in the *Book of the Duchess* (160–65):

> Save ther were a fewe welles
> Came rennynge fro the clyves adoun,
> That made a dedly slepynge soun,
> And ronnen doun ryght by a cave
> That was under a rokke ygrave
> Amydde the valey, wonder depe.

---

[37] *BD* 982.   [38] *CT* B². 4314.   [39] *CT* B². 3325–6.
[40] Ibid. 3405–6.   [41] Ibid. 3557–9.   [42] Ibid. 3585.

St Neophytos[43] was born near Larnaca in Cyprus in 1134. At his cave-hermitage, a series of chambered caves near Paphos in western Cyprus, he attracted a community of followers. From this cave (or 'Enkleistra' as he called it) he withdrew to a more secluded one higher up the slopes of the same hill. He wrote many works including one called 'Concerning the calamities that have fallen on Cyprus' in which he described the conquering of the island by Richard Cœur de Lion in 1191. Like the Wife of Bath's fourth husband

> Al is his tombe so curyus
> As was the sepulcre of hym Daryus,
> Which that Appelles wroghte subtilly.[44]

St Neophytos in fact dug his own grave and made his own coffin (or *cheste* as Chaucer would have called it).

St Neophytos's Enkleistra, like the 'temple of myghty Mars' in *The Knight's Tale*,

> Al peynted was the wal, in lengthe and brede.[45]

In the 'nave' (south wall), Abraham and his wife Sarah entertain three angels by offering them dinner; on the western wall, twelve saints, bearded and austere, St Anthony, St Andronikos, St Makarios, and others; on the north wall, the enthroned Christ; on the roof, a painting of the Ascension; elsewhere, representations of Christ washing the disciples' feet, the Agony in the Garden, Christ standing before Pontius Pilate, the Crucifixion, the Deposition, and the Resurrection.

In Western European terms none of this is remarkable in itself—such places of pilgrimage and saintliness are scattered throughout Europe—and yet because of its very remoteness, its sacredness, and its frescoes, I felt in a curious way closer to the world of Chaucer than when walking in the streets of modern London or visiting Canterbury Cathedral.

King Peter of Cyprus, conqueror of Alexandria, was added to

---

[43] See C.G. Christodoulides, *Saint Neophytos Monastery: History and Art* (Nicosia, 1980); A. and J.A. Stylianou, *The Painted Churches of Cyprus* (Cyprus,? Nicosia, 1964).

[44] *CT* D. 497–9.

[45] *CT* A. 1970.

Chaucer's list of illustrious men as an example of the power of Fortune:

> Thus kan Fortune hir wheel governe and gye,
> And out of joye brynge men to sorwe.[46]

St Neophytos would not have qualified for *The Monk's Tale*, because he never descended 'fro wele unto wo' but, had Chaucer known of him, he would have fitted easily enough into one of Chaucer's numerous other frames.

VI

Troilus and Cressida was also written by a Lombard Author; but much amplified by our *English* Translatour, as well as beautified; the Genius of our Countrymen in general being rather to improve an Invention than to invent themselves; as is evident not only in our Poetry, but in many of our Manufactures.[47]

Thus the verdict of Dryden at the turn of the eighteenth century. Four centuries earlier no tradition had established itself of analysing the virtues of contemporary poets. Instead they were simply proclaimed. A thin layer of eloquent praise survives from medieval times—encomiums by Deschamps, Gower, and Usk. In his *Ballade to Chaucer* (?1386) Deschamps links Chaucer with the ancients:

> O Socratès plains de philosophie,
> Seneque en meurs et Auglus en pratique,
> Ovides grans en ta poëterie
> Briés en parler, saiges en rethorique.[48]

In the *Confessio Amantis* (? 1390) (VIII. 2941–49) Venus addresses Gower:

> And gret wel Chaucer whan ye mete,
> As my disciple and mi poete:
> For in the floures of his youthe
> In sondri wise, as he wel couthe
> Of Ditees and of songes glade,

---

[46] *CT* B². 3587–8.
[47] John Dryden, Preface to *Fables Ancient and Modern* (1700), ed. J. Kinsley (1962), p. 526.
[48] *Mod. Lang. Notes* (1918) XXXIII. 269.

> The whiche he for mi sake made,
> The lond fulfild is overal:
> Whereof to him in special
> Above alle othre I am most holde.[49]

And in his *Testament of Love* (? 1387) Thomas Usk declared:

> In goodnes of gentil manliche speche, without any maner of
> nycetè of storiers imaginacion, in witte and in good reson of
> sentence he passeth al other makers.
>
> (Bk III, Ch. 4.)[50]

There is nowhere else to turn for a literary estimate in the fourteenth
century, except for the self-deprecatory remarks of Chaucer himself:

> That Chaucer, thogh he kan but lewedly
> On metres and on rymyng craftily,
> Hath seyd hem in swich Englissh as he kan.[51]

This hierarchical mode of judgment has inevitably been applied to
Chaucer ever since, perhaps most memorably in the following three
extracts:

> Chaucer, I confess, is a rough Diamond, and must first be polish'd
> e're he shines. —Dryden (1700)[52]

> And yet, I say, Chaucer is not one of the great classics. He has not
> their accent . . . Something is wanting, then, to the poetry of
> Chaucer, which poetry must have before it can be placed in the
> glorious class of the best. And there is no doubt what that some-
> thing is. It is the $\sigma\pi o\upsilon\delta\alpha\iota\acute{o}\tau\eta\varsigma$, the high and excellent serious-
> ness, which Aristotle assigns as one of the grand virtues of poetry.
> —Arnold (1888)[53]

> Chaucer wrote while England was still part of Europe. There was
> one culture from Ferrara to Paris and it extended to England.
> Chaucer was the greatest poet of his day. He was more compend-
> ious than Dante. —Ezra Pound (1934)[54]

---

[49] In G.C. Macaulay's EETS edition (1900).
[50] Cited from W.W. Skeat, *Chaucerian and Other Pieces* (Oxford, 1897),
p. 123.
[51] *CT* B¹. 47–9.
[52] Ed. J. Kinsley (1962), p. 533.
[53] *Complete Prose Works* (1973) IX. 176.
[54] *ABC of Reading* II. 87.

In the twentieth century Chaucer has been taken over by academic writers. Preposterous hidden meanings have been discovered in his works as if he were a theologian in disguise. His vocabulary has been weighed in every conceivable set of scales, for its innovatory power, its aptness to the rhymes, its semi-veiled rudeness, the proportions of Gallic and of native words, and the distribution of words that preserved or had acquired a final -e. Many words still remain impenetrably obscure in meaning or derivation, for example *cankedort* and *vitremyte*. The identity of the pilgrims has also remained unsolved despite the exhaustive detective work of J.M. Manly and his adherents. Every wart and tuft of hair of the pilgrims has been assigned an inferential meaning.

But notwithstanding all this noble scholarship, the tribes of heroes and villains that Chaucer drew from his 'olde bokes' were captivatingly different from any others of his own day or of ours. They cannot be properly understood except by prolonged study of the tribes that preceded them and from whom they were derived.

In all that has been written about Chaucer, no one disputes that from 'Here bygynneth the Book of the Tales of Caunterbury' to 'And you shal have absolucion', the first and last words in the standard edition of Chaucer's works, a world of different realms is encompassed, approximately accurate, stupendously enjoyable, and as poetically powerful as that of any English writer up to the time of William Shakespeare.[55]

[55] I am indebted to Mrs. L.S. Burnett, Miss E.A. Knight, and Miss E.M. Knowles for help of various kinds in the preparation of this article; and to Mrs. A.E. Singer for typing it.

II

The Poet and Taboo: The Riddle of Shakespeare's 'Pericles'

JOHN PITCHER

I

At present, it would seem that there are only two things one should not do when writing about *Pericles*: find fault with the hero, and find anything of interest in the first two acts. I had better say straight away that in this essay I propose to do both of these things. This is not as perverse as it seems. Admittedly, the text of the play is corrupt beyond repair, but even so it is possible to detect a continuity between Acts I and II and III to V, and a continuity which is related to the danger, or *periculum* in Pericles himself. This is scarcely the first claim for an integrity in *Pericles*, and it would be a grave disservice to Wilson Knight, Edwards, and others not to acknowledge how much has been done to disclose the unity of the play. None the less, one can still read, in quite a recent book,[1] that in *Pericles* 'there is a pattern which does not start till the storm at the beginning of the third act', and that the marriage at the end of Act II 'concludes the bad part of the play'. It is this attitude in particular which I shall try to contest.

Whether or not they are Shakespeare's,[2] the first two acts of *Pericles* are not as negligible as critical orthodoxy suggests. It is true that in certain places the verse is very poor, but there is a distinct achievement in structure, for the dramatist has wrought a sense out of the shapeless sequence of adventures offered in the sources. In the first scene, Prince Pericles of Tyre risks his life in attempting to win the daughter of Antiochus, King of Antioch. He does not know that Antiochus has enticed his daughter to incest, enticed her to an 'evil should be done by none'. If he is to win the girl, Pericles must answer a riddle proposed by the king: if he fails to interpret it (as many other

---

[1] Frank Kermode, *William Shakespeare: The Final Plays* (London, Longman, for the British Council, 1973), pp. 13–14.

[2] The question of authorship is discussed by Philip Edwards in his Penguin edition, *Pericles Prince of Tyre* (Harmondsworth, 1976), pp. 31–41. All my quotations from *Pericles* are taken from this edition.

suitors have), he must lose his life. When the princess appears, Pericles, in an ecstasy of admiration, describes her as 'apparelled like the spring,/Graces her subjects', and with 'inflamed desire' in his breast, he longs

> To taste the fruit of yon celestial tree
> Or die in the adventure . . .
>
> (I.i.22–23)

The connections between death, sexual desire, and the fruit of a tree have an unmistakable resonance. The tree of knowledge and death in Eden also brought with it a new awareness of sexuality. And perhaps it is this, the notion of man and wife as sexual partners (even ones fallen from *grace*) which provokes Antiochus, the incestuous father, to divert the associations away from Eden to the gardens of Hesperus. For the king, his daughter is a classical, not a biblical figure. In reply to Pericles, he says:

> Before thee stands this fair Hesperides,
> With golden fruit, but dangerous to be touched,
> For deathlike dragons here affright thee hard.
>
> (I.i.28–30)

Editors have quite often noted that there is an allusion in this to Hercules and his eleventh labour, but what has not been stressed is that the Hesperides were the guardians of the apples, or 'golden fruit', which Juno received on the day she married Jupiter. In other words, the daughters of Hesperus protected the wedding gift and symbol of a lawful love between married partners. In Antioch, by contrast, 'this fair Hesperides', the king's incestuous daughter, has certainly not protected the sanctity of her parents' union. The ironies in these speeches, picking open the web of incest, are not anticipated in the sources, no more than are the frequent connections, initiated here, between death, a child, physical attraction, and the act of eating. The importance of this conjunction centres on the riddle itself, where the incest is ravelled into paradoxes. The daughter declares:

> *I am no viper, yet I feed*
> *On mother's flesh which did me breed.*
> *I sought a husband, in which labour*
> *I found that kindness in a father.*
>
> (I.i.65–68)

In this the child feeds on her mother, and (by a suggestive pun on 'labour') seeks and begets her father, finding in him the 'kindness' (gentleness *and* sexual nature) of a husband. What matters here is that the incest can no longer be contained within one flesh, one bed of darkness, one regal city. Pericles recoils from it in horror, and flees from Antioch to Tyre, and then on to Tarsus, but there is no escape across the seas from such knowledge. In every place that he visits, the same configuration of child, death, sexual attraction and eating will reappear, in however disguised a form. This at least is what I think is intended in the descriptions, in I.iv, of Tarsus, the city Pericles relieves with his shiploads of corn. In this place, not long before the famine, there had been great wealth, arrogance, and an emphasis on smart good looks:

> For riches strewed herself even in her streets,
> Whose towers bore heads so high they kissed the clouds,
> And strangers ne'er beheld but wondered at,
> Whose men and dames so jetted and adorned,
> Like one another's glass to trim them by;
> Their tables were stored full, to glad the sight,
> And not so much to feed on as delight . . .
>
> (I.iv.23–29)

Less than two years later, not only has the concupiscence disappeared, but 'man and wife/Draw lots who first shall die to lengthen life', and those mothers who

> to nuzzle up their babes
> Thought naught too curious are ready now
> To eat those little darlings whom they loved.

In the sources for *Pericles*, there is of course a famine at Tarsus which the hero relieves, but there is no precedent for this constellation of death, eating flesh, physical attractiveness and contact between mother and child. The link between the incest of Antioch and the famine of Tarsus is made still clearer in the single line describing the city's buildings:

> Whose towers bore heads so high they kissed the clouds.

Primarily this must refer to the tall and vaulting skyline of Tarsus, but it cannot but remind us, grimly, of the suitors who had tried in vain to solve the incestuous riddle, and whose heads were left impaled on the walls of Antioch.

In Pentapolis, on whose shores Pericles is shipwrecked in Act II, the bonding between food and desire is met with once more, and again in the company of a father and daughter. After Pericles has vanquished the other knights in the tournament, he is feasted as the victor, but even as they admire his honourable bearing, his future wife (Thaisa) and father-in-law (Simonides) connect his physical appearance to the food before them. In an aside, Simonides confesses (II.iii.28–29):

> By Jove, I wonder, that is king of thoughts
> These cates resist me, he but thought upon

and at the same moment Thaisa says to herself (30–32):

> By Juno, that is queen of marriage,
> All viands that I eat do seem unsavoury,
> Wishing him my meat . . .

Here the delicacies are unpalatable because Thaisa would prefer Pericles as her 'meat': later in the scene, when her father, Simonides, toasts the prince's health, he wishes the wine to be 'so much blood' in the young man's veins (75–77). Perhaps even the references to Jupiter and Juno, in these apparently casual avowals, are to be traced back to Antioch and the allusion to the Hesperides, the guardians of the nuptial gifts which Juno received on her wedding day. In the court at Pentapolis, Pericles is again, as in Antioch, put to a test which endangers his life (albeit the trial is ritualized into a tournament), and again a king attempts to trap him in a daughter's words, though here the snare is a letter rather than a riddle (II.v.40–71). Throughout these scenes, Pericles' 'courage' (physical bravery *and* sexual ability) is continually being tested by a father who approves of his daughter's love for the prince, but who seems as jealous and forbidding as Prospero with Miranda and Ferdinand. On other occasions, Simonides can descend almost to pandering his child to the young stranger (and this anticipates the brothel scenes in Mytilene). Before we accept him as a benign, generous father—the complete antithesis to Antiochus—we should recall his crude sexual puns and behaviour as he brings Pericles and Thaisa together in the dance:

> Come, sir, here's a lady that wants breathing too,

And I have heard you knights of Tyre
Are excellent in making ladies trip,
And that their measures are as excellent.

(II.iii.100–104)

In short, though Simonides is contrasted with Antiochus in several respects, his conduct as a parent does not extinguish the memory or the sin of that incestuous father. I think his tests, his deceit, and his bawdiness are intended to create in us the uneasy feeling that not all is well at the end of Act II.

II

In these acts I am not claiming that there is an especially sophisticated development of this incest motif. But I do think that there is an intelligence at work here, even if it is not Shakespeare's intelligence, which has tried to organize the narrative as a sequence which signals the keynote of incest in Antioch, extrapolates it in Tarsus, and leaves it provocatively unresolved in Pentapolis. The movement is confirmed further by symmetries in structure. In I.ii, Pericles is afflicted by (to him) an inexplicable melancholy after he has interpreted the riddle: in II.iii, in the court of Simonides, he suffers an even more surprising melancholy amid the joyful revelling. In the first instance, he has to overcome his revulsion at the bond of incest between a father and daughter, while in the second, immediately before his betrothal, he is about to separate Thaisa from her father.

Where I would differ from a critic like Ernest Schanzer[3] is in seeing these early adventures as part of an order. Not an order established by the gods, or Providence, or Lady Fortune, but one which is inextricably connected back to the crime in Antioch. However far Pericles travels, and whatever the immediate cause of his adventures (shipwreck, etc.), the incestuous union will reassert itself, in varied forms, until it is extirpated (in marriage, as it seems at the end of Act II). For Schanzer, and several other critics, the play throughout is a series of accidents and misfortunes without design, which demonstrate the 'undeserved sufferings of the wholly innocent and entirely virtuous'. In Acts III–V, so this argument runs, Pericles and his daughter Marina are subject to chance adversity and random good

---

[3] See Schanzer's introduction to his edition of *Pericles* in *The Complete Signet Classic Shakespeare*, gen. ed. Sylvan Barnet (New York, Harcourt Brace Jovanovich, 1972), pp. 1407–15.

fortune. Separated from one another by the seas, treacherous foster-parents, and pirates, they respond in different ways, and with different strengths to their trials. In total, it is the parallels and contrasts between father and daughter which 'give shape and coherence to the episodic and formless romance on which *Pericles* is based'.[4]

My objection to this approach is that it ignores or undervalues the continuation of the theme of incest from the first two acts into the final three. As I see it, the marriage of Pericles and Thaisa at the end of Act II has resolved only one aspect of the lingering, festering consciousness of Antiochus' crime: the hero has been freed into sexual consummation with a wife. Antiochus and his daughter have been horribly destroyed by the gods, leaving only the stink of their reputation and their charred flesh,[5] but the violation is not something simply to be left in the past. Even in the moment of begetting Marina (at the beginning of Act III), a new proximity between father and daughter is engendered, and one which is potentially dangerous. Dangerous because, after the supposed death of Thaisa, this parent and child are separated and become strangers to each other. Marina is left in Tarsus with Cleon and Dionyza, and when she grows into a beautiful and talented young girl, her foster-mother plans to have her murdered. The plot goes awry, she is captured by pirates, and eventually she ends up in a brothel in Mytilene. Her father, having remained in the city of Tyre until her adolescence, journeys to Tarsus, only to be told (falsely, of course) that she has died. Cast apart thus, these characters would appear to be lost to one another for ever, and yet we are aware that, ineluctably, like opposing poles of a magnet, they will be drawn together once more (as they are in Act V). The potential danger in their separation, however cautiously we wish to express it, is that their reunion will not be a happy one. The danger is that Pericles, wandering without purpose and believing that his child is dead, may (by chance) arrive in the brothel in which Marina is still imprisoned, and there, unknowingly, purchase and enjoy his own daughter as an enforced whore. The pattern which began in Antioch, when he encountered and knowingly rejected an incestuous daughter, would then be closed, locked tight, into a tragic symmetry. This underlying danger never surfaces as explicitly as this account of it, but its shape and its menace are clear enough. It has the symmetry of the most famous of incestuous tragedies, the story

---

[4] Schanzer, p. 1412.
[5] II.iv.2–15. Pericles does not learn of their destruction until later; see Gower's chorus (21–25) before Act III.

of Oedipus. Indeed, there are several ways in which the medieval romance of Apollonius (the ultimate source for *Pericles*)[6] rearranges, adapts and inverts elements from the classical story. Oedipus, we recall, solves the riddle of the Sphinx, but is unable to discover the reason for the plague which is destroying his new city, Thebes. Apollonius (and Pericles) also solves a riddle, but unlike Oedipus he is able to see that it is his own presence which threatens his kingdom (and accordingly he leaves Tyre before Antiochus can attack it). The stories are even more closely related if one considers how conscious the heroes are of the danger carried within them. Fearful of the prophecy that he will kill his father and mate with his mother, Oedipus flees *knowingly* from his adoptive parents: *unknowingly* he murders his father at the crossroads, and begets children by his mother, Jocasta. In this medieval variation, Apollonius flees knowingly from the evil of incest, but he may, all too easily and unconsciously, participate in the very crime he had abhorred, sexual intercourse with a daughter.

It may be objected that *Pericles* is not a tragedy, whatever connections there are between its source and the story of Oedipus, and further that there is no evidence of the hero's coming anywhere near the brothel in Mytilene (even though he does land there in Act V). We may begin an answer to this if we consider Northrop Frye's definition of Menandrine New Comedy, the comic structure used by Shakespeare throughout his career. This, so Frye tells us,

> unfolds from what may be described as a comic Oedipus situation. Its main theme is the successful effort of a young man to outwit an opponent and possess the girl of his choice. The opponent is usually the father (*senex*) . . . [who] frequently wants the same girl, and is cheated out of her by the son, the mother thus becoming the son's ally. The girl is usually a slave or courtesan, and the plot turns on a *cognitio* or discovery of birth which makes her marriageable. Thus it turns out that she is not under an insuperable taboo after all but is an accessible object of desire . . . Often the central Oedipus situation is thinly concealed by surrogates and doubles of the main characters . . .[7]

[6] See Geoffrey Bullough, *Narrative and Dramatic Sources of Shakespeare* (London and Henley, Routledge and Kegan Paul, 1977 reprint), VI, pp. 351–3.

[7] 'The Argument of Comedy' quoted here from *Shakespeare's Comedies: An Anthology of Modern Criticism*, ed. Laurence Lerner (Harmondsworth, Penguin Books, 1967), p. 315.

Pericles has frequently been described as an experimental play, but if we think of it in Frye's terms, several elements can be regarded as permutations on this well-established New Comic structure. The characters involved are Pericles himself, the *senex*, Marina, the involuntary courtesan, and Lysimachus, the governor of Mytilene and eventually Marina's husband. The setting for their conflict is the whorehouse in Mytilene. Pericles does not visit the brothel in person, of course, but there is considerable evidence that when, in IV.vi, his future son-in-law Lysimachus does, it is as a thinly concealed surrogate or double for the main character, Pericles. In simple terms, we need not think of Pericles actually in presence in the brothel for there to be this danger of the incestuous tragic symmetry closing in Mytilene. There is, as it were, a pressure from Pericles in this scene, even though he is off stage, and indeed wandering the Mediterranean at the very moment Lysimachus first sets eyes on Marina.

III

Evidence for identifying Lysimachus with Pericles varies from single lines to large questions of dramatic propriety. But the possibility that the characters were in some way linked first occurred to me when reading one of the sources for the play, Laurence Twine's novel, *The Pattern of Painful Adventures*. In Twine's account of the episodes in Mytilene, there is a detail which enlightens us about both Lysimachus' age, and his substitution or doubling for a father. In the brothel, when the Marina-figure is brought in to the disguised governor, she moves him to compassion by recounting her misfortunes. To comfort her, he says:

> Be of good cheere . . . for surely I rue thy case, and I my selfe have also a daughter at home, to whome I doubt that the like chances may befall

and, again, when the girl pleads with him not to reveal her story he answers:

> No surely . . . unlesse I tell it unto my daughter, that she may take heede when she commeth unto the like yeares, that she fall not into the like mishappe: and when he had so saide, he let fall a fewe teares, and departed.[8]

[8] Quoted from Bullough, p. 457.

In the source, then, Lysimachus is probably an older man, and Marina's sexual degradation makes him fearful for his own child. Twice Marina's sorry state reminds him that he is a father, and we must assume that he sees in her the daughter he has left at home. In the play there is none of this. Rather than accept him as an actual father, Shakespeare changes the governor into a younger (and more eligible) suitor, and one who will substitute for a parent. If we read his character in these terms, then even seemingly casual remarks will assume a more disquieting importance. Consider, for example, the exchange between the Bawd and Lysimachus when Marina is first brought to him:

> BAWD   Here comes that which grows to the stalk, never plucked yet, I can assure you.
>
> *Enter Boult with Marina*
>
> Is she not a fair creature?
>
> LYSIMACHUS   Faith, she would serve after a long voyage at sea . . .
>
> (IV.vi.37–41)

Edwards glosses the final line as a 'coarse expression of admiration: she's just the girl a sex-starved sailor would be delighted to meet'.[9] Hoeniger, on the other hand, reads it as 'a sardonic remark, belittling the Bawd's praise; all the more ironic in a play about voyages'.[10] It is indeed ironic, but the irony is more specific than this, surely, for the one thing which has characterized Pericles is *his* long voyages at sea. This scene was written by Shakespeare in his late period, and it would be unusual if such a line, which introduces a man to his future wife, did not resonate throughout the play. It reminds us, inexorably, of the father about to return from his sea journeys. Another kind of evidence might be grouped under the heading, *the disguised suitor*. Such a motif first appears in II.i, when Pericles meets the fishermen after his shipwreck (a scene often attributed to Shakespeare). In this episode, the fishermen drag up the armour which belonged to Pericles' father, and the hero arms himself in it, even though it has rusted in the sea water. He goes to the court in Pentapolis, as an unknown knight of low degree, and there wins his bride, Thaisa. He is disguised in the sense that no one knows his

[9] Edwards, p. 180.
[10] *Pericles*, ed. F.D. Hoeniger (London, Methuen, Arden Shakespeare Paperback, 1969), pp. 127–8.

identity or rank, and he is possessed not only of his father's armour, a physical protection, but also his *amour*, his sexual prowess. (So much is clear from the puns on *arms* in Simonides' speech, II.iii.94–98.) In the brothel scene in IV.vi it is not Pericles who is the disguised suitor, but rather Lysimachus. The governor comes in disguise to win Marina, and offers to put aside his office if she will surrender to him—'I protest to thee, pretty one, my authority shall not see thee.' Clearly Lysimachus has come to the whorehouse with a very impatient sexual desire, and in view of the analogous episode in Pentapolis, and the notion there of an absent father infusing a son with physical and sexual energy, there may well be a parallel with the absent Pericles and his 'son' Lysimachus. It is also relevant that at this stage of the action, Pericles too is disguised, since his hair and beard have not been cut for fourteen years. This disguise was assumed in Tarsus, when he vowed that his hair would remain unscissored until Marina was married (III.iii.27–30). His unshorn hair, by tradition signifying strength and sexual virility, will thus conceal *his* identity for as long as his daughter is without a husband.

The most significant connections between the men are made by Marina in the way she first speaks to each of them. When in V.i she is brought to the barge in the hope of curing a stranger's melancholy, she sings to him. He does not respond, and when she urges him to listen, he pushes her away from him. At once she reveals, but only cryptically, that her derivation is 'from ancestors/Who stood equivalent with mighty kings', even though misfortune has now reduced her to servitude. There begins an exchange of questions from Pericles, and answers from Marina which seem like riddles. He asks if she were born in Mytilene, and she replies:

> No, nor of any shores,
> Yet I was mortally brought forth, and am
> No other than I appear.
>
> (V.i.102–104)

At this point in one of the sources, the Marina-figure poses a set of three riddles for her father.[11] These he easily deciphers in turn as referring to the sea, a sailing-ship, and a 'bath and hoathouse' (the Elizabethan euphemism for a brothel). Thus they are all allusions to the combined experiences of a father and daughter, and they are intended to recall the incest-riddle set in Antioch (which also encodes

---

[11] Bullough, pp. 465–6.

the experience all too closely shared by a parent and child). In *Pericles*, Shakespeare transmutes these formal riddles into Marina's cryptic, puzzling speeches which her father eventually interprets, but only with difficulty. Noticeably, Marina speaks in a comparable way in only one other place: in the brothel when Lysimachus questions her about her sexual experience:

> Now, pretty one, how long have you been at this trade?
> What trade, sir?
> Why, I cannot name it but I shall offend.
> I cannot be offended with my trade. Please you to name it.
> How long have you been of this profession?
> E'er since I can remember.
> Did you go to't so young? Were you a gamester at five, or at seven?
> Earlier too, sir, if now I be one.
>
> (IV.vi.62–71)

The quibbles on 'trade' and 'profession' appear elsewhere in the brothel scenes, but in this case they anticipate the riddling, half-revealing manner in which Marina will speak to her father in Act V. The parallels here are of the utmost importance. Lysimachus is unable to unravel her speech because, in terms of the play's structure, he has come to the brothel as a disguised, ambiguous figure. Is he simply a young man whose reformation will make him a suitable husband for Marina? Or is he a surrogate for Pericles, the father whose sexual presence must not repeat the crime of Antiochus? When in Act V Pericles is able to make sense of his daughter's answers, it is because he appears as himself, as a father deep in melancholy at the loss of a child. Twice before he has suffered this melancholy, once because of the horror of Antioch, and once before he became a husband to Thaisa. On this third occasion, precisely because his surrogate has been resisted in the brothel, he discovers Marina as a father, not an aroused suitor, nor a husband-to-be. In my view, this is why the play is a comedy and not a tragedy. Lysimachus does finally win the girl, but only (as I read it) when he is no longer a substitute doubling for Pericles. The tragic symmetry which threatened to close by proxy in the brothel is avoided, and there-after the main characters are united and reunited according to the principles of New Comedy.

There is no way in which one can establish that Shakespeare thought of the play in these terms, even if the author's intention is accepted as a relevant critical issue. Yet one can observe that substitution, which is so important in, say, *All's Well That Ends Well* and *Measure for Measure*, operates explicitly in one area of *Pericles*. While the hero is away from Tyre on his many adventures, his counsellor Helicanus rules the city in his stead. Much is made of Helicanus' loyalty and good service, and when Pericles finally discovers Thaisa in Ephesus, he introduces her to him with these lines:

> You have heard me say, when I did fly from Tyre,
> I left behind an ancient substitute.
>
> (V.iii.50–51)

Since Helicanus was an *ancient substitute* for Pericles in his role as the Prince of Tyre, it is not difficult to conceive of Lysimachus as a *youthful* substitute for him in the illicit sexual advances in Mytilene.

IV

It would be possible to accumulate further evidence in this way, but perhaps enough has been said already to alter *some* of our thinking about Lysimachus. Critics have differed in their estimate of the governor's role, some of them dismissing it entirely, others arguing that it is at the heart of the play. Schanzer, for example, concludes that

> Marina exists primarily not in relation to a lover but to her father. She is given a husband at the end, but in a most perfunctory way, and we are never even told whether she loves him. Shakespeare is clearly not at all interested in the Marina–Lysimachus relationship.[12]

For Philip Edwards, however, the contrast between the governor and afflicted princess is 'in many ways the hub of the whole play', even though, in the text as we have it, Lysimachus is an impossibly contradictory figure. In his edition of the play, Edwards has made the problem quite clear.[13] When Lysimachus comes to the brothel at the beginning of IV.vi, he is no more than another customer, joking rather coarsely with the bawds, and keen to have a healthy whore. Marina is presented to him, and after a few brief exchanges, she

---

[12] Schanzer, p. 1413.
[13] Edwards, pp. 21–6 (from which the quotations in this paragraph are taken).

laments her state. Quite suddenly he says 'Had I brought hither a corrupted mind,/Thy speech had altered it', he gives her gold, and he assures her (106–108):

> For me, be you thoughten
> That I came with no ill intent; for to me
> The very doors and windows savour vilely.

As Edwards notes, this is a moment of great importance, but one which leaves us rather confused about Lysimachus' intentions. Are we to think of him as a prince who has no thought of violating Marina, and who has come only to test her virtue? Or is this encounter 'an image of the purification of a man who sins through thoughtlessness'? If we accept the first option, that Lysimachus imposes an ordeal on Marina, it makes him 'quite revoltingly callous and cruel', however many parallels we draw with the tests set by Prospero, and by the Duke in *Measure for Measure*. Conversely, if we conclude that he is purified in the brothel, then the Quarto must have omitted whole passages of Marina's saving eloquence.

Whatever their differences, Edwards and Schanzer are both right about Lysimachus. It is difficult to regard him as psychologically consistent or morally acceptable as a suitor, or to find much importance in his role as Marina's husband (in the final scene, V.iii, he is not even given a single speech). My own feeling would be that such questions assume too readily that his character is important in itself. If I am right in describing him as an ambiguous substitute for Pericles, a kind of sexual amphibian, then the contradictions in his identity will matter much less. Rather than worry about the two (or three) images of Lysimachus which are blurred in the defective text, it might be more appropriate to focus his inconsistent behaviour on Pericles. Marina and Pericles have been described by one critic as the *double focus* of the play, Marina has frequently been contrasted with Antiochus' daughter, and even the conduct of the two fathers, Antiochus and Simonides, has been thought worthy of comparison. The silence about Pericles and Lysimachus may indicate just how successfully the incest taboo works outside as well as within the play.

Much of my case rests on a distortion of reality, since I am arguing that a man on the high seas can also be present (at least in his surrogate) in the city of Mytilene. Such a distortion is possible because of the nature of Shakespearean Romance. In the late plays, as

Northrop Frye has remarked,[14] Shakespeare seems to have gone out of his way to create impossible circumstances (such as Thaisa's revival, or the passage of fourteen years in a chorus of a few minutes). These impossibilities in the plot, which are self-evident, prepare us, by working on our susceptibilities, for strange patterns of a less evident kind. It seems to me that in *Pericles* such impossibilities loosen the normal stringency imposed on identity (Thaisa is dead and not dead), and allow the father and son to converge in the climactic assault on Marina. It is difficult to imagine how the danger of incest could have been dramatized in any other manner. In the source for *The Winter's Tale*, Greene's *Pandosto*, there is an episode in which the Leontes-figure is guilty of overt (albeit unknowing) incestuous desire. In Philip Edwards' words,

> Leontes (to call the characters by the names they have in the play) becomes infatuated with his daughter Perdita, neither knowing who the other is. Though ashamed of such desire at his age, he tries to win her from Florizel by persuasion and threats and make her his concubine. She resists him. When he later learns that the girl he has pursued is his own daughter, 'calling to mind . . . that contrary to the law of nature he had lusted after his own daughter . . . he slew himself.'[15]

Shakespeare excises all of this, of course, because it has no place in the design of *The Winter's Tale*. It is also the kind of episode which easily degenerates into melodrama (as it does in *Pandosto*), and the suicide of a guilty father would hardly fit into a comic structure. So even in *Pericles*, where a father's desire for a daughter *is* of thematic import-ance, we should not expect an incestuous encounter to be dramatized explicitly. Instead, the subject is figured and refigured in the imagery of Acts I and II, and then prolonged, as far as possible, into the structure of III, IV and V. There may be a discontinuity of technique in these two sections (perhaps suggesting divided authorship), but there is a continuity of *attention* to the theme of incest. If we see this as sustained across the play, and especially in the brothel scenes, then there is even more force to the argument, propounded by C.L. Barber,[16] that Marina rebegets her father, or creates him anew, in

[14] *A Natural Perspective: The Development of Shakespearean Comedy and Romance* (New York, Columbia University Press, 1965), pp. 18–21.

[15] Edwards, p. 32.

[16] ' "Thou that beget'st him that did thee beget": Transformation in *Pericles* and *The Winter's Tale*', *Shakespeare Survey*, XXII (1969), pp. 59–67.

Act V. In their reunion, she is not simply contrasted with Antiochus' daughter (as several critics have suggested): rather, in Mytilene she has prevented the crime of the past threading its symmetry into the future.

To say the least, I have emphasized already the continuing importance of Antioch in *Pericles*, but perhaps I may propose one small, final articulation of the incest motif. If we consider the riddle itself, Antiochus' daughter is depicted as mother, wife, and child to her father. Is it possible that this triple identity is given counter-expression, once more in varied form, in the goddesses who are invoked throughout the play? We observe how many times the characters make vows to Diana, appeal for Lucina's aid, and refer to Juno, and so perhaps we should remember that (on good classical authority) these deities were identified with one another. Juno, goddess of marriage, was sometimes called Lucina (goddess of childbirth), as was Diana, goddess of chastity. They were thus linked together as the guardians of the mother in labour. In *Pericles*, Thaisa avows her love by Juno, gives birth at sea with aid implored from Lucina, and enters the temple of Diana after her 'death' and revival.[17] Her daughter Marina, so assisted by Lucina, is described as 'in pace another Juno', and as a 'maid-child' who wears Diana's 'silver livery'.[18] Are these conjunctions merely fortuitous, or are they aligned to certain changes of name from the sources? In Twine's novel, Thaisa is called Lucina, and her daughter is Tharsia. In the play, the names shift along from daughter to mother, and from mother to goddess of childbirth. But though the patron goddesses of mother, wife and unmarried daughter are so linked, they are not confused and confined in one flesh. Within Antiochus' child, though her father says of her that Lucina reigned at her birth, it is obvious that the roles, and times, appointed for each of the goddesses have coalesced into one:

> *He's father, son, and husband mild;*
> *I mother, wife, and yet his child.*

> (I.i.69–70)

In one tradition, the Hesperides, with whom she is compared were three daughters: in Antioch, this one daughter has become three— mother, wife and child. As the play develops, and the symmetries of

[17] II.iii.30–32; III.i.10–14; III.iv.8–14.
[18] V.i.111; V.iii.6–7.

incest first threaten to close, but then do not, the goddesses are an invoked accompaniment as the mother who is Pericles' wife, and the daughter who is not, are reunited in Ephesus, separate but not separated figures.[19]

[19] I wish to thank Dr Robert Welch for his judicious and illuminating comments on a draft of this essay. I am of course entirely responsible for the views expressed here.

III

The Appropriation of Milton

BERNARD SHARRATT

I

I said to people here at Cambridge: in the thirties you were passing severely limiting judgements on Milton and relatively favourable judgements on the metaphysical poets, which in effect redrew the map of seventeenth-century literature in England. Now you were, of course, making literary judgments—your supporting quotations and analysis prove it, but you were also asking about ways of living through a political and cultural crisis of national dimensions. On the one side, you have a man who totally committed himself to a particular side and cause, who temporarily suspended what you call literature, but not in fact writing, in that conflict. On the other, you have a kind of writing which is highly intelligent and elaborate, that is a way of holding divergent attitudes towards struggle or towards experience together in the mind at the same time. These are two possibilities for any highly conscious person in a period of crisis—a kind of commitment which involves certain difficulties, certain naïvetés, certain styles; and another kind of consciousness, whose complexities are a way of living with the crisis without being openly part of it. I said that when you were making your judgments about these poets, you were not only arguing about their literary practice, you were arguing about your own at that time. The reaction to this was scandalized denial that anything so tainted could have entered into the critical process.

Raymond Williams's remarks, in an interview with the editors of *New Left Review* in 1977,[1] indicate one basic difficulty in tracing and assessing the impact of Milton on subsequent generations: the inextricability (however frequently disavowed) of political and literary judgments. Thirty years earlier, T.S. Eliot, reflecting upon his own and Samuel Johnson's criticisms of Milton, admitted the difficulty:

[1] Raymond Williams, *Politics and Letters* (London, New Left Books, 1979), pp. 335–6.

The fact is simply that the Civil War of the seventeenth century, in which Milton is a symbolic figure, has never been concluded. The Civil War is not ended: I question whether any serious civil war ever does end. Throughout that period English society was so convulsed and divided that the effects are still felt. Reading Johnson's essay one is always aware that Johnson was obstinately and passionately of another party. No other English poet, not Wordsworth, or Shelley, lived through or took sides in such momentous events as did Milton; of no other poet is it so difficult to consider the poetry simply as poetry, without our theological and political dispositions, conscious and unconscious, inherited or acquired, making an unlawful entry.[2]

Eliot's curious final phrase anticipates the later 'scandalized denial' Williams records, for what is at stake for Eliot as for those Cambridge critics is the very possibility of regarding 'the poetry simply as poetry'.[3] It is at least doubtful if Milton himself would have accepted Eliot's formulation, yet, ironically, Milton's own poetry has been perhaps the crucial reference-point, in England, for precisely that notion of 'poetry' as an activity sublimely separate from all other concerns. An investigation of that apparent paradox may link and illuminate the areas this essay proposes to explore: the influence of Milton upon later readers, his own conception of 'the poet', and the role of Milton's work in the development of that deeply ideological practice we now call 'literary criticism'.

The entangled history of the reception and reputation of Milton over three centuries obviously cannot be summarized here,[4] but some significant continuities can be indicated. As Mark Pattison noted, in 1879,

Milton's repute was the work of the Whigs. The first édition de luxe of Paradise Lost (1688) was brought out by a subscription got

[2] T.S. Eliot, On Poetry and Poets (London, Faber & Faber, 1957), p. 148.
[3] Eliot makes this problem explicit in the 'Note' to section II of his 1929 essay on Dante, Selected Essays (London, Faber & Faber, 1961), pp. 269–70.
[4] Cf., for example, W.R. Parker, Milton's Contemporary Reputation (Ohio State University Press, 1940); Milton: the Critical Heritage, ed. J.T. Shawcross (London, Routledge & Kegan Paul, 1970); Milton Criticism: Selections from Four Centuries, ed. J. Thorpe (London, Routledge & Kegan Paul, 1951); The Romantics on Milton, ed. J.A. Wittreich (Cleveland/London, Case Western Reserve University Press, 1970); James G. Nelson, The Sublime Puritan: Milton and the Victorians (Madison, University of Wisconsin Press, 1963).

up by the Whig leader, Lord Somers. . . . It was the Whig essayist, Addison, whose papers in the *Spectator* (1712) did most to make the poem popularly known. In 1737, in the height of the Whig ascendancy, the bust of Milton penetrated Westminster Abbey, though, in the generation before, the Dean of that day had refused to admit an inscription on the monument erected to John Phillips, because the name of Milton occurred in it.[5]

One conservative response to this Whig adulation, already apparent in the 1690s, was to concede, even applaud, Milton's stature as author of *Paradise Lost* while counterposing the poetry to the prose, as if either the poem redeemed the politics or the pamphlets merely spoiled our appreciation of the poet—as in the reactions of Oldys and Yalden respectively:

> The bard, who next the new-born saint addrest,
> Was Milton, for his wondrous poem blest;
> Who strangely found, in his Lost Paradise, rest.
>   'Great bard', said he, ' 'twas verse alone
>   Did for my hideous crime atone,
>   Defending once the worst rebellion.'[6]

> These sacred lines with wonder we peruse,
> And praise the flights of a seraphic muse,
> Till the seditious prose provokes our rage,
> And soils the beauties of thy brightest page.[7]

Two centuries later, Pattison's own biography of Milton reproduces this divorce between the prose and the poetry on another level, in its explicit organization and in its basic preferences:

Milton's life is a drama in three acts. The first discovers him in the calm and peaceful retirement or Horton, of which *L'Allegro, Il Penseroso*, and *Lycidas* are the expression. In the second act he is breathing the foul and heated atmosphere of party passion and religious hate, generating the lurid fires which glare in the battailous canticles of his prose pamphlets. The three great poems, *Paradise Lost, Paradise Regained*, and *Samson Agonistes*, are

---

[5] Mark Pattison, *Milton* (London, Macmillan, 1890), p. 217.

[6] Alexander Oldys, 'An Ode by Way of Elegy on . . . Mr Dryden' (1700), in Shawcross, op. cit., p. 124.

[7] Thomas Yalden, 'On the Reprinting of Milton's Prose Works' (1698), in Shawcross, op. cit., p. 122.

the utterance of his final period of solitary and Promethean grandeur.[8]

During the second act:

> He was writing not poetry but prose, and that most ephemeral and valueless kind of prose, pamphlets, extempore articles on the topics of the day. He poured out reams of them, in simple unconsciousness that they had no influence whatever on the current of events.[9]

Both Garnett and Raleigh soon criticized Pattison for perpetuating this split, but George Whiting, writing in 1939, still had to propose a connection between the pamphlets and *Paradise Lost* as if his were a novel and tentative suggestion:

> Literary critics who ignore backgrounds and who insist upon treating poetry as merely an esthetic product have as a rule neglected or condemned Milton's work and interests in the period from 1640 to 1658, which they regard as an unfortunate episode in the life of the poet. Even those who do not deplore his activities in this middle period and who regard his prose as a powerful but unbalanced expression of his genius often fail to observe any relationship between the prose and the later poems . . . [nevertheless] It is probable that *Paradise Lost* . . . is related more intimately than has been realized not only to Milton's prose but also to the political–religious interests that engrossed the middle period.[10]

One might easily interpret Eliot's notorious recommendation, three years earlier, that *Paradise Lost* itself should be read twice, 'first solely for the sound, and second for the sense',[11] as yet another variation on this long-established divorce between the 'prose' and the 'poetry' in Milton.

Whiting's book, as a contribution to 'Milton scholarship', utilized the prose primarily as a quarry to elucidate the poems. The long lineage behind such scholarship stretches back to Patrick Hume's

---

[8] Pattison, op. cit., p. 14.
[9] Ibid., p. 169.
[10] G.W. Whiting, *Milton's Literary Milieu* (University of North Carolina Press, 1939, reissued by Russell & Russell, New York, 1964), pp. 218–19.
[11] *On Poetry and Poets*, p. 143.

'Annotations' of 1695,[12] and his almost unprecedented treatment of a near-contemporary text as if it were a Greek or Latin classic requiring and justifying scholarly commentary was followed by Bentley's 1732 edition of *Paradise Lost*, with a textual apparatus and editorial attitude that again accorded the poem 'classical' status. By the late nineteenth century, *Paradise Lost* had become, quite literally, the equivalent of a Latin text within the educational practices of the public schools: the Clarendon Commission of 1864 recorded that, at Shrewsbury, 'fourth-formers who were excused from studying Ovid's *Fasti* were expected to memorize about twelve hundred lines from Milton.'[13] The Taunton Commission, a few years later, was told how pupils at a Liverpool school

> took passages from Milton, read them backwards and forwards, and put them into other order, and they were obliged to parse them and explain them. The same faculties were exercised there in construing Milton as in construing Latin.[14]

F.R. Leavis presumably had such educational practices at least partly in mind when he complained in 1936 that 'however admirable' Milton's own prose and verse written in Latin 'may be judged to be, to latinize in English is quite another matter, and it is a testimony to the effects of the "fortifying curriculum" that the price of Milton's latinizing should have been so little recognized.'[15]

Criticism of Milton's 'latinizing' goes back to Addison, and beyond,[16] but Addison's main contribution to Milton's reputation was, of course, to develop and popularize the emphasis of Dennis and others on Milton's 'sublimity', thereby bequeathing to the

---

[12] Cf. A. Oras, *Milton's Editors and Commentators from Patrick Hume to Henry John Todd, 1695–1801* (London, Oxford University Press, 1931). Some established 'scholarly' approaches to Milton have been usefully criticized in Robert M. Adams, *Ikon: John Milton and the Modern Critics* (New York, Cornell University Press, 1955), especially Chapters III and V. Pattison considered that 'An appreciation of Milton is the last reward of consummated scholarship', *Milton*, p. 215.

[13] R.D. Altick, *The English Common Reader* (Chicago and London, University of Chicago Press, 1963), p. 181.

[14] Ibid., p. 185.

[15] F.R. Leavis, *Revaluation* (Harmondsworth, Penguin), p. 50.

[16] T.S. Eliot, *On Poetry and Poets*, p. 153, quotes Samuel Johnson's 'most important censure of Milton', which in turn quotes Addison's phrase, 'Our language sunk under him.'

eighteenth century one of its key terms and dominant influences. It was not, however, only the argument—and the unusual length—of Addison's criticism in the *Spectator* articles that shaped eighteenth-century responses to Milton. By devoting his *Saturday* essays to Milton, Addison indicated and encouraged the suitability of *Paradise Lost* for Sunday reading,[17] and throughout the eighteenth and nineteenth centuries Milton's poem shared the privileged and widely influential status of 'Sunday book' with those other 'Puritan' texts, *Pilgrim's Progress* and *Robinson Crusoe*. Q.D. Leavis, lamenting in 1932 the demise of this domestic practice, commented:

> The difference that the disappearance of the Sunday book a generation ago has made, its effect on the outlook and mental capacity of the people, would repay investigation.[18]

A specific topic for investigation in the case of *Paradise Lost* is indicated by T.H. Huxley's complaint, recorded by Pattison, that deeply engrained popular conceptions of cosmogony, so resistant to scientific enlightenment, derived from *Paradise Lost* Book VII rather than from *Genesis* itself. Pattison himself claimed, even more radically yet quite convincingly, that 'most English men and women would probably have some difficulty in discriminating in recollection' what they had derived from Milton and what from the Bible concerning the whole story of the Creation and Fall.[19]

Yet it was not only ordinary households of an Evangelical cast which accorded *Paradise Lost* a special status. The various designations in the eighteenth century of Satan as the 'hero' of the poem, according to the 'rules' of epic, were transmuted by Blake and Shelley into a political reading of the poem which was inherited by the radical working class of the nineteenth century, while Milton's own political commitment to the Commonwealth was re-emphasized in the context of Chartist struggles. The *Chartist Circular* for 13 March 1841 carried a glowing account of Milton as 'an honest, unflinching stern Republican', who 'valiantly fought for civil and

---

[17] A point made by Patrick Parrinder, *Authors and Authority: a Study of English Literary Criticism and its Relation to Culture 1750–1900* (London, Routledge & Kegan Paul, 1977), p. 11.

[18] Q.D. Leavis, *Fiction and the Reading Public* (London, Chatto & Windus, 1968), p. 117.

[19] Pattison, *Milton*, pp. 184, 189. Readers who experience this difficulty can now consult the excellent work by J.M. Evans, *Paradise Lost and the Genesis Tradition* (Oxford University Press, 1968).

religious liberty, against the tyranny of Charles I'; but it is worth noting that Milton's life and prose writings are given priority in the article over the poetry, with *Paradise Lost* summarized in a single paragraph.[20] The *Northern Star* for 5 July 1845 advertised twelve lectures by the recently imprisoned Thomas Cooper, beginning with 'Ancient Egypt' and ending with 'prospects of the future'; the entire ninth lecture was to be on 'Milton: his patriotism and poetry etc.'.[21] Cooper himself records that he had, by the age of thirteen, 'read the "Paradise Lost"; but it was above my culture and learning, and it did not make me *feel*, though I read it with interest, as a mere story.'[22] One wonders how many working-class readers of, for example, the eighteen 'cheap serial' numbers of *Paradise Lost* published in 1825–6 had the same reaction.[23]

II

Clearly, these mere indicators of Milton's impact and reputation represent only a highly selective fragment of the whole, while the direct and indirect influence of Milton upon English literature is, obviously, pervasive and incalculable.[24] My examples, however, illustrate the extent to which Milton's work has been appropriated within each of the crucial social and ideological institutions of English society: educational, religious, domestic and political. That *Paradise Lost* should be memorized by public schoolboys, recommended to radical Chartists, selected as suitable Sunday reading by Christian households, applauded by Whig politicians and encased in

[20] The essay is reprinted in *An Anthology of Chartist Literature*, ed. Y.V. Kovalev (Moscow, 1956), pp. 299–302. Cf. also A.K. Stevens, 'Milton and Chartism', *Philological Quarterly*, XII (1933), pp. 377–88.

[21] The advertisement is given in full in John Saville's Introduction to *The Life of Thomas Cooper Written by Himself* (1872) (Leicester University Press, 1971), pp. 18–20.

[22] *The Life of Thomas Cooper Written by Himself* (London, Hodder & Stoughton, 1872), p. 35.

[23] Cf. Louis James, *Fiction for the Working Man 1830–1850* (Harmondsworth, Penguin University Books, 1974), p. 89. James notes (p. 113) that Milton even appeared as a character in J.F. Smith's 'immensely popular' penny issue historical novel *Stanfield Hall* (1849–50).

[24] Cf., for example, R.D. Havens, *The Influence of Milton on English Poetry* (Cambridge, Harvard University Press, 1922). For some interesting indications of Milton's indirect influence upon a significant branch of English prose fiction see David Punter, *The Literature of Terror: a history of Gothic Fictions from 1765 to the present day* (London, Longman, 1980, *passim*).

scholarly commentaries, at least underlines its peculiar status. Some explanation of that extraordinary position might be approached by briefly considering Milton's own practice as a writer in relation to the social and ideological institutions of the seventeenth century.

Any summary of Milton's various pronouncements on the nature of a 'poet' and on his own conception of his 'calling' would result in a complexly overdetermined definition, drawing upon elements inherited from or paralleled in Sidney, Spenser, Jonson and, behind them, Plato, Aristotle, Quintilian, Cicero, Horace and the Bible: the poet as orator, teacher, statesman, creator, prophet.[25] A different but complementary approach would recognize that almost every text, whether 'prose' or 'poetry', produced by Milton prior to the publication of *Paradise Lost* bears traces of some contextual situation, of a relationship to a postulated and particular audience within some social or institutional setting, and in many cases those traces indicate more than a merely textual convention. When Milton constructs the *Areopagitica* as a classical oration delivered to 'the Parliament of England' or addresses himself to 'the Lords and Commons' in *The Doctrine and Discipline of Divorce*, the rhetorical device embodies a real social practice which the text transposes: Milton is, at one level, actually appealing to the Parliament as legislators who may indeed be persuaded. Even as late as February 1659 the rhetorical gestures indicate a genuine and specific attempt at intervention:

> I have prepared, supreme Council, against the much expected time of your sitting, this treatise . . . in a season wherein the timely reading thereof to the easier accomplishment of your great work may save you much labour and interruption.[26]

Similarly, a great deal of the poetry can be assigned to particular occasions or socially functional practices: school exercises, elegies

---

[25] There is a usefully compressed account by Isabel Rivers, 'The making of a seventeenth-century poet', in *John Milton: Introductions*, ed. J. Broadbent (Cambridge University Press, 1973), pp. 75–107.

[26] *A Treatise of Civil Power in Ecclesiastical Causes*, preliminary address 'To the Parliament'. For convenience of reference I have quoted from John S. Diekhoff's invaluable volume, *Milton on Himself* (London, Cohen & West, 1965), p. 177, following his modernizations. Subsequent references will be to Diekhoff and to the Columbia Milton, *The Works of John Milton*, gen. ed. Frank A. Patterson (New York, Columbia University Press, 1931–40), 20 volumes, abbreviated to CM.

and epitaphs, commemorative volumes, complimentary verses, celebrations, entertainments, devotions, epistles. Reading Milton's early poems one is aware of the poet not only adopting but in many cases actually performing particular social roles; it can even seem (almost) sensible to consider whether Milton really did attach Sonnet VIII ('Captain, or colonel, or knight in arms') to his door to disarm a potential Cavalier assault! As J.S. Smart noted in this case, 'we are in the presence of a poetical situation, not of a practical expedient',[27] but the distinction he makes is often far less applicable. Underpinning any notion Milton may have had of 'the poetry simply as poetry'—in Eliot's phrase—is an active awareness of a range of practical uses of writing, of the various functions of particular writing practices as embodying and reinforcing Milton's relations to others as teacher, friend, correspondent, propagandist. Even when Milton formulates what might seem a purely 'aesthetic' notion, the underlying Platonic conception indicates that the primary aim is fundamentally philo- sophical-theological, even devotional, as in the letter to Diodati of 23 September 1637:

> What besides God has resolved concerning me I know not, but this at least: He has instilled into me, if into anyone, a vehement love of the beautiful . . . it is my habit day and night to seek for this Idea of the beautiful, as for a certain image of supreme beauty, through all the forms and faces of things (for many are the shapes of things divine) . . .[28]

When Henry Oldenburg suggested to Milton, in 1654, that his talents might be more worthily employed than in replying to the *Cry of the Royal Blood* Milton's response reveals rather different criteria from those Pattison, for example, would approve:

> To prepare myself, as you suggest, for other labours—whether nobler or more useful I know not, for what can be nobler or more useful in human affairs than the vindication of liberty?—truly . . . I shall be induced to *that* easily enough . . . not that in any way I repent of what I have done, since it was necessary; for I am far from thinking that I have spent my toil, as you seem to hint, on matters of inferior consequence.[29]

[27] J.S. Smart, *The Sonnets of Milton* (Glasgow, Maclehose, Jackson, 1921), p. 57.
[28] Diekhoff, p. 125, CM, XII, p. 27.
[29] Diekhoff, p. 136, CM, XII, p. 65.

It is, indeed, in the prose writings concerned with 'the vindication of liberty', and not just in the poetry, that we find Milton appealing for or implying divine assistance and inspiration, and it has been plausibly suggested that Milton, by 1654, saw himself as having fulfilled his task of writing a national epic in, precisely, his authorship of the *Defensio*.[30] When any form of writing is recognized as performing a function over and essentially above any strictly 'literary' satisfaction, the distinction between 'the prose' and 'the poetry' is far from primary.

But for a text to perform a particular social purpose effectively it must not only postulate but actually reach and influence its appropriate audience, and by August 1659 Milton is clearly unsure of his readership, as the opening paragraphs of *The Likeliest Means to Remove Hirelings* indicates:

> to whom should I address what I still publish . . . but to you ['supreme Senate', Parliament] . . . and to whom more appertain these considerations which I propound than to yourselves and the debate before you, though I trust of no difficulty, yet at present of great expectation, not whether ye will gratify (were it no more than so) but whether ye will hearken to the just petition of many thousands . . . or whether ye will satisfy . . . the covetous pretences and demands of insatiable hirelings

—and so, rather sadly, on.[31] By October 1659 Milton can only write a *Letter to a Friend concerning the Ruptures of the Commonwealth*—but the 'friend' was perhaps only a fiction, the *Letter* remained unpublished till 1698, and Milton himself admits to 'not finding that either God or the public required more of me than my prayers for them that govern'.[32] In the conclusion to the *Ready and Easy Way to Establish a Free Commonwealth*, of February 1660, as the 'restoration' loomed ever closer, Milton can barely pretend that he speaks to any actual audience, except, 'with the prophet', to the very stones—and to God Himself—and, perhaps, to the future.[33] The appeal to Urania, in the invocation to Book VII of *Paradise Lost*, must, by then, have seemed, if anything, over-optimistic:

---

[30] Cf. Diekhoff, pp. 222, 239.
[31] Diekhoff, p. 179, CM, VI, pp. 43 f.
[32] Diekhoff, p. 183, CM, VI, p. 101.
[33] Diekhoff, p. 246, CM, VI, p. 148.

still govern thou my song,
Urania, and fit audience find, though few.

III

It is, of course, a familiar argument that *Paradise Lost* can be read as Milton's theological attempt to make sense of the defeat of the 'good old cause' of God's own 'saints'. Since he had, to the very last, continued to believe in God's providential guidance of the political fate of the Revolution—even claiming the restoration of the Rump Parliament in May 1659 as 'a new dawning of God's miraculous providence among us' and calling upon God to 'suffer not' the final Restoration in *A Ready and Easy Way*[34]—Milton, faced with the actual crushing fact of the Restoration, had somehow, still, to re-assert 'Eternal Providence' and 'justify the ways of God'—if only to himself. To adapt Marx: Milton could now only attempt to understand, no longer to change, his world. But to do so involved not only speaking for God but also, in a sense, to God, as A.D. Nuttall has recently argued.[35] One might even suggest that Milton, in reciting the tale of mankind's fall and Christ's heroic redemption, finally assumes the traditional role of the epic poet, the court bard, he had once outlined in *Ad Patrem* (lines 41–49): he sings the exploits of his true and only king in the very presence of that king, a presence that takes the most intimate form of inspiration. But, in more mundane terms, the choice of the epic form, that anachronistic, timeless mode, indicates that Milton is no longer writing within or for any immediate social purpose or occasion: this poem is not a political intervention but a theological inquiry, albeit an inquiry into the very deepest roots of political possibility itself. One can indeed interpret *Paradise Lost* as probing the most fundamental reasons of all for the defeat of God's 'saints', by associating that issue with the fiercely problematic nature of man's disobedience to God's will and with the desperately difficult question of the conditions for the final establishment of God's own kingdom; but such a cosmic extension of the immediate dilemma necessarily precludes any directly effective human rectification of the present political disaster. All that one could be required to do, as a post-Restoration reader of *Paradise Lost*, would be to acknowledge one's own participation in its overall

[34] Diekhoff, pp. 179, 246; CM, VI, pp. 43, 148.
[35] A.D. Nuttall, *Overheard by God: Fiction and Prayer in Herbert, Milton, Dante and St John* (London, Methuen, 1980).

scenario of Fall and Redemption—and reform *oneself* accordingly.

But what is then interesting is how this absence of any immediately practical purpose or specific audience opens up the possibility of quite alternative ways of reading *Paradise Lost*. Not only Milton himself but, in various ways, all the opposing participants in the struggles of 1640–60 had sought for the intelligibility and justification of their political actions and fates in overtly theological categories. By the early eighteenth century this was no longer the case, for a variety of interlocked reasons which can only be cursorily noted here. One central factor was a change in the relations and respective powers of what Althusser terms the 'ideological apparatuses'. An index to this basic shift would be that whereas in the 1630s the liaison between the Court and the Church endowed Archbishop Laud with decisive authority, by the reign of Queen Anne 'it caused a sensation when, for the last time, a Bishop was appointed to government office'.[36] Another, related, facet of the change is that while the Civil War could certainly be seen by its participants as a conflict of large social and ideological forces, with divine intervention and interest claimed by all sides, for the generation which read the *Spectator* the crucial reference-point was 1688 not 1649 and both the constitutional settlement of 'the Glorious Revolution' and the subsequent jostlings and local manoeuvrings of 'Whigs' and 'Tories' seemed easily amenable to explanations far less grandiose, and far less noble, than the direct attentions of the Godhead. More generally, one could claim that by the time Addison praised *Paradise Lost* the very notion of a seriously applied *theological* explanation of the defeat of a political principle or party must have seemed extremely remote, and even quaint. An appeal might still be made, of course, to the benevolent oversight of the Deity upon British affairs ('God Save the King') and the relevance of religious allegiance to the constitutional fate of James II was clear—but the change in ideological atmosphere has made theological explanations and vindications of political events seem increasingly redundant and perhaps even unintelligible in themselves. Indeed, something of that change is already apparent by the 1680s: when the preachers and pamphleteers of the 1640s characterized their opponents as 'sons of Belial' they intended a far more literal application[37] than, for example, Dryden did in writing,

---

[36] Christopher Hill, *The Century of Revolution 1603–1714* (London, Sphere, 1969), p. 14.

[37] Cf. Whiting, op. cit., Ch. VI.

in 1681, of Lord Shaftesbury as 'Achitophel'.

If, however, by the 1700s the strictly theological dimension of *Paradise Lost* is no longer recognizable or even intelligible as a serious reaction to a specific political dilemma, the poem itself still required and prompted a response—and in Addison's treatment, above all, we can see taking shape not merely a reading of the poem 'as literature' but almost the very emergence of that notion of 'literature', we have inherited. In broad terms, one could suggest that while Milton himself transposed his political dilemma into a theological form, Addison's essays transformed *Paradise Lost* from a theological inquiry into a 'literary' narrative, to be read primarily for its 'literary' qualities and secondarily, perhaps, as suitable devotional (not theological) matter for a Sunday. This is not, of course, to say that *Paradise Lost* had not been responded to as a text with 'literary' qualities before Addison, but only that the eliding of any substantially theological or political significance of the poem in Addison's strictly 'literary' criticism encapsulates, concentrates and bequeaths to subsequent readers a notion of 'literature' as, precisely, defined by its distinction from 'non-literary' considerations which Milton would not himself have wholeheartedly endorsed. Addison's immensely influential essays on Milton did indeed become paradigmatic for the development of the allied notions of 'literature' and 'criticism' which underpin today's profession of 'literary criticism'. It would take this essay too far afield to analyse Addison's role in that development in relation to his own political and ideological position[38] or to trace the full significance of his conception of 'literature' in the subsequent consolidation of an ideological notion of 'culture' in England, but a few concluding pointers can be given.

By the time of Macaulay's *Edinburgh Review* article on Milton, in August 1825—ostensibly a review of the recently discovered *De Doctrina*—the idea that Milton's own theology might be at all relevant to *Paradise Lost* can be casually acknowledged and perfunctorily disposed of in a sentence, while the lack of awareness of any substantial political dimension of the poem is apparent in Macaulay's use, for example, of a story from Ariosto concerning a 'foul' and 'loathsome' snake, without ever adverting to its resound-

---

[38] Cf., for example, the interesting suggestions in L.A. Elioseff, 'Joseph Addison's Political Animal: Middle Class Idealism in Crisis', *Eighteenth Century Studies*, VI, no. 3 (Spring 1973), pp. 372–81.

ing echoes of the problem of Satan's role in *Paradise Lost*.[39] For Macaulay, Milton's stature and reputation as a 'great poet' merely makes him extremely useful as a culturally prestigious ornament to claim for one's own party. Some forty years later, Matthew Arnold's proposal that 'culture' and 'literature'—of which Milton is by then a supreme exemplar—might finally take the place of religious belief in our lives must seem the most perverse twist in this history of the appropriation of Milton. But that honour, one can also claim, is reserved for Eliot and Leavis who, in effect, came close to treating *Paradise Lost* not as itself an attempt to understand the course of history in the seventeenth century but rather as itself part of the 'explanation' of what, for them, crucially 'happened' in that century: in the notion that 'a dissociation of sensibility set in'—the major evidence for which is Milton's work—we can see the extraordinary substitution of 'literary history' and 'cultural' explanation for both theological and political ways of making sense of history itself. For Eliot's own 'theology of history' we have to go, of course, to *Four Quartets*.

IV

This overcompressed account only suggests an argument that would need to be elaborated at considerable length. Clearly, the overall development I have sketched is influenced by many other factors and is exceedingly complex, but the role of *Paradise Lost* as a central reference-point within that development can, I think, be connected back to its status as a theological response to a political situation. Once the text became dissociated from its context and its 'literary' qualities divorced from its political and theological dimensions it could be appropriated as simply devotional reading, literary 'classic' or scholarly-critical fodder. Yet the text still carried its political and theological charge, most obviously in its treatment of Satan's rebellion, and those seriously concerned with either politics or theology, whether nineteenth-century Chartists or twentieth-century Christians and atheists, have, necessarily, recognized that to treat this poem 'simply as poetry' is to avoid its full challenge.

[39] Macaulay writes: 'Such a spirit is Liberty. At times she takes the form of a hateful reptile. She grovels, she hisses, she stings. But woe to those who in disgust shall venture to crush her! And happy are those who, having dared to receive her in her degraded and frightful shape, shall at length be rewarded by her in the time of her beauty and glory!' *Critical and Historical Essays* (London, Longmans, Green & Co., 1877), p. 19.

It seems appropriate that a generation of politically radical critics (in the wake of the 'defeat' of 1968?) have recently turned their attention to Milton;[40] it is clear, once again, that the 'civil war' is still being fought out over Milton, not least in the ideological battles over the very nature of 'literature' and 'criticism' at his own university.[41] With a nice sense of irony one marxist critic has even taken Eliot's and Leavis's criticisms of Milton and argued that the features they deplore are precisely those which a 'revolutionary criticism' derived from Benjamin and Derrida should exploit.[42]

An even deeper irony has, however, to be recognized in conclusion. It was a chaplain of King George IV who finally edited the De Doctrina in 1825, at His Majesty's command; in 1841 Prince Albert commissioned William Etty's Comus paintings for the garden pavilion of Buckingham Palace; and in 1981, at the wedding of the future King Charles III of England, it was a text by Milton that was sung while the happy couple signed the register.[43] 'Simply as poetry', as a purely aesthetic or merely devotional experience, Milton's work can still so easily be appropriated by those against whom he fought.

---

[40] See, for example, the essays on Milton by David Aers and Gunther Kress, Anthony Easthope, and Fredric Jameson, in 1642: Literature and Power in the Seventeenth Century, 'Proceedings of the Essex Conference on the Sociology of Literature', ed. Francis Barker et al. (University of Essex, 1981); Allen Grossman, 'Milton's Sonnet "On the Late Massacre in Piedmont"': a note on the Vulnerability of Persons in a Revolutionary Situation', Literature in Revolution, ed. C. Newman and G.A. White (Boston, Holt, Rinehart and Winston, 1972), pp. 283–301; Michael Wilding, 'Regaining the Radical Milton', The Radical Reader, ed. S. Knight and M. Wilding (Sydney, Wild & Woolley, 1977), pp. 119–44; Robert Hodge, 'Satan and the Revolution of the Saints', Literature & History, No. 7 (Spring 1978), pp. 20–33; Andrew Milner, John Milton and the English Revolution: a study in the sociology of literature (London, Macmillan, 1981); and, of course, C. Hill, Milton and the English Revolution (London, Faber and Faber, 1977).

[41] Of those most prominently involved in recent disputes within the Cambridge English Faculty, Professor C. Ricks has written Milton's Grand Style and Dr C. MacCabe is currently researching a book on Milton.

[42] Terry Eagleton, Walter Benjamin or Towards a Revolutionary Criticism (London, New Left Books, 1981), pp. 3–13.

[43] For Etty's paintings, see M.R. Pointon, Milton and English Art (Manchester University Press, 1970), pp. 208–12. The text sung at the Royal Wedding, 29 July 1981, was from Handel's Samson, 'Let the Bright Seraphim', adapted by Handel's librettist from Milton's 'At a Solemn Music', lines 10–13.

Pope's Waste Land: Reflections on Mock-Heroic

CLAUDE RAWSON

'An Epic Poem, the Criticks agree, is the greatest Work Human Nature is capable of'.[1] So said Martinus Scriblerus in Pope's *'Receipt to make an* Epic Poem'. The words are cited verbatim in Pope's Scriblerian gloss on *Dunciad*, IV. 174. The critics did indeed 'agree'. The thing was a commonplace, and like other commonplaces it was much repeated by Dryden, most ringingly when he ushered in his translation of the *Aeneid* with words which differ from those of Pope's boorish and undisciplined pedant mainly in their avoidance of the unmannerly final preposition: 'A heroic poem, truly such, is undoubtedly the greatest work which the soul of man is capable to perform'.[2]

Pope's 'capable of', used on both occasions, is a tell-tale sign, for although the words occur in an *Art of Sinking in Poetry* or the mock-commentary to a mock-epic, Pope is mocking neither the sentiment, nor Dryden, nor epics. He was not given, like his friend

---

[1] *The Art of Sinking in Poetry (Peri Bathous)*, ed. E.L. Steeves (New York, Russell & Russell, 1968), p. 80. The 'Receipt' had first appeared, in a slightly different form, in *Guardian*, No. 78, 10 June 1713. Quotations from Pope's poems use the Twickenham Edition (TE) text throughout, except in the case of the mock-editorial paraphernalia of *The Dunciad*'s four-book or B version of 1743 (the one normally cited here), which is from the *Poetical Works*, ed. Herbert Davis, introd. Pat Rogers (Oxford, Oxford University Press, 1978). This is because TE does not give a full continuous text of this editorial material in the form in which it appeared in 1743. This essay is in part an attempt further to develop some notions in my book *Henry Fielding and the Augustan Ideal Under Stress* (London, Routledge, 1972), where fuller documentation on some points touched on here is to be found.

[2] *Of Dramatic Poesy and other Critical Essays*, ed. George Watson (London, Dent, 1962), II. 223; also I. 198, II. 96 (hereafter cited as Watson). For Rapin's expressions of this view, see *Essays of John Dryden*, ed. W.P. Ker (Oxford, Clarendon Press, 1900), I. 313; for others, see William K. Wimsatt and Cleanth Brooks, *Literary Criticism. A Short History* (New York, Knopf, 1957), pp. 197–8.

Swift, to jeering at Dryden. If Dryden was in his mind at all, it was probably as the best-known recent authority against the barbarism of ending sentences with 'of'. Dryden had spoken in 1672 of such final prepositions as an example of the unpolished nature of Elizabethan English, unworthy of a more refined age.[3] It is likely, however, that Pope just used the rather crude example as a self-evident solecism, signalling the character of his speaker rather than questioning the intrinsic truth of the statement.[4] The targets of his ridicule are vulgar pedants uttering sacred truths by rote, without literacy or comprehension, and poetical hacks like Blackmore, scaling heroic heights, according to receipt, *'without a Genius*, nay without Learning or much Reading'.[5] The proposition itself, that an epic was the noblest product of the human mind, was accepted by Pope as unreservedly as by Dryden. It was indeed so securely taken for granted that he could afford to put it in the mouth of a foolish and derided speaker without fear of being misunderstood.

A century of so later, as is well known, Mill and Poe and others were saying that an epic poem, 'in so far as it is epic . . . is not poetry at all', that a long poem was 'simply a flat contradiction in terms', that 'no long poem was ever written; the finest long poem in the world being but a series of short poems linked together by prose'.[6]

[3] Dryden admits having committed the fault himself (Watson I. 174). He took steps to correct it in the second edition of the *Essay of Dramatic Poesy* (Watson, I. 174 n. 4 and see I. 13 n. 3, I. 23 n. 4: for many further examples, see the footnotes to the *Essay*, passim, in the California Dryden, vol. XVII). H.W. Fowler, *Dictionary of Modern English Usage*, 2nd edn rev. Sir Ernest Gowers (Oxford, Clarendon Press, 1965), pp. 473–4, cites Dryden as the chief authority, with Gibbon, for the objection to final prepositions.

[4] In practice and especially in informal contexts Pope, like most speakers of English (including Dryden), himself committed the supposed solecism, e.g. *Correspondence*, ed. George Sherburn (Oxford, Clarendon Press, 1956), I. 57, 108 (the first, oddly, from a letter which contains one of Pope's rare censures of Dryden).

[5] *Art of Sinking*, p. 80.

[6] M.H. Abrams, *The Mirror and the Lamp* (London, Oxford University Press, 1960), pp. 23–4, 136–7; Arthur Symons, citing Poe's authority, *The Symbolist Movement* (London, Constable, 1911), p. 134. The chief texts are Mill's 'What Is Poetry?' and Poe's 'The Poetic Principle'. One of Mill's formulations gets the older valuation of epic in by a side door: 'an epic poem, though in so far as it is epic (*i.e.* narrative) it is not poetry at all, is yet esteemed the greatest effort of poetic genius, because there is no kind whatever of poetry which may not appropriately find a place in it' (*Literary Essays*, ed. Edward Alexander, New York, Bobbs-Merrill, 1967, p. 60).

The notion that poetry can only be sustained in brief charged moments is still our normal assumption, and we forget that the short poem has not always been regarded as the principal or most characteristic vehicle of poetic expression. Dryden tended to reserve the word 'poem' for grander things than 'a paper of verses' or 'ordinary sonnet'.[7] The French, 'light and trifling' in both language and genius, are more fitted 'for sonnets, madrigals, and elegies than heroic poetry',[8] and Boileau's famous line, 'Un sonnet sans défauts vaut seul un long Poëme' (*Art Poétique*, II. 94), might seem to confirm Dryden's view of this frivolity.[9] But the assertion is less wholehearted than it sounds, and Boileau says that no one has yet achieved such a sonnet anyway ('cet heureux Phénix est encore à trouver'). He is not asserting the superiority of sonnet to epic, but preferring a small-scale perfection to the long and tedious, or to work more ambitious but botched. He mocked the failure of modern French attempts at epic, as Dryden noted 'the failings of many great wits amongst the Moderns, who have attempted to write an epic poem',[10] or as Pope ridiculed Blackmore and others in the 'Receipt', *The Dunciad* and elsewhere.

A well-known paradoxical aspect of this was that epics on classical models were often written by those who seemed least committed, and scorned by those most committed, to the values of the classical past. This commitment, for Pope, was no mere abstraction. The vitality of his reverence for ancient epic is visible not only in his critical writings on Homer, but also whenever he engages with the epic masterpieces in his own poems. In the *Essay on Criticism*, Pope imagines the young Virgil, at first unconcerned with rules or models, scorning the critic's law and drawing only from nature's fountains:

---

[7] Watson, I. 87. Sonnet, for Dryden, is likely to have meant any short poem.

[8] Watson, II. 238. Mill also, for different but not unrelated reasons, thought the French were 'the least poetical of all great and intellectual nations' (*Literary Essays*, p. 57).

[9] Boileau's 'long Poëme' seems to refer mainly to bad epics. In the nineteenth-century discussions, 'epic' and 'long poem' were also sometimes interchangeable, and in a sense what was deemed by Poe to be wrong with epic is precisely that it was extended. The older opposition to epic by certain authors in Hellenistic and Roman times (Callimachus, Martial, Juvenal), sometimes involved considerations of length, though on different grounds.

[10] Gordon Pocock, *Boileau and the Nature of Neo-Classicism* (Cambridge, Cambridge University Press, 1980), pp. 109 ff.; Watson, II. 85.

But when t'examine every Part he came,
Nature and Homer, were, he found, the same.

(ll. 134–35)

The last line is much cited as a pithy formulation, and Pope repeated its substance in critical prose.[11] But the real force of the passage is in the spare vibrant finality, the feeling of excited recognition, as of an old truth suddenly become vivid. Virgil's discovery about Homer is also Pope's own, not in any sense which relates to the biographical progress of either poet, but in the poetic now of its setting down. It would be hard to imagine anything further removed from mere critical lip-service to an ideal which had lost its creative force.

There is a second paradoxical fact, also familiar. The high view of epic survived, with greater or less vitality, throughout the lifetimes of Dryden, Pope, and Fielding, and indeed beyond. Perhaps it has never fully disappeared. And yet there is no major epic in English nor perhaps in any of the main West European languages after Paradise Lost. Both Dryden and Pope planned, as Milton had deliberately planned from an early stage, to write epics of their own. Pope in particular began his poetic career by publishing the Pastorals, thus signalling a Virgilian promise of greater things. But neither Dryden nor Pope achieved their epics. Part of the epic impulse, adulterated by romance elements and generally coarsened, was diverted, by Dryden and others, into the heroic play, a genre which was quickly seen by many as a further example of the failure of the heroic mode to animate genuinely good writing. It became a target for parody from The Rehearsal to Fielding's Tragedy of Tragedies, much as many modern epics were parodied and derided. Some recent critics believe that Dryden himself was subverting certain features of the heroic outlook in his plays.[12]

Dryden's one completed and successful attempt at epic was the translation of Virgil, as Pope's was the translation of Homer. It was as though they could only do it by proxy, or through a filter of irony. Boileau said he wished someone would write a new Aeneid to celebrate French triumphs in war, and that he sometimes toyed with the idea himself, but found he could not because his own bent was satirical (A.P., IV, 203–36; Ep., VIII. 1–12). But Blackmore did what

[11] 'Postscript to the Odyssey', TE, X. 389.
[12] See Derek Hughes, Dryden's Heroic Plays (London, Macmillan, 1981), pp. viii and 168–9 n.3, for a convenient listing of such views.

Dryden had merely talked of doing, and produced not one but two Arthurian epics. Dryden said, 'I will deal the more civilly with his two poems, because nothing ill is to be spoken of the dead', but Blackmore continued undeterred.[13] Pope was to refer to him as one 'whose indefatigable Muse produced no less than six Epic poems' (*Dunciad*, II. 268 n.). Bad poets writing epics were an upstart modern arrogance, a desecration of ancient altars, and above all an awful warning of dangers amusingly codified in Pope's 'Receipt'; while good poets, like Boileau or Pope, unable to write epic straight nor yet to leave it alone, wrote mock-epics.

The unease to which this testifies was, in this period, a creative force. It animates the great mock-heroic poems of the Augustan age, and underlies the prose style of Fielding and others. But it begins in England with *Paradise Lost*, not a mock-heroic in any ordinary sense. This last great classical epic bears no direct relation to any 'heroic age', any more than the *Aeneid* does. But unlike those nineteenth-century poems by Tennyson or Morris whose evocation of the heroic was largely a matter of nostalgia for 'a world that no longer exists and . . . values that have passed away',[14] *Paradise Lost* retains a live (though 'secondary' or 'literary') relation to the epic tradition. The imaginative grandeurs embodied in the great epics were for Milton, as they had been for Virgil, a focus of aspiration sufficiently rich and active to provide a form for expressing some high pre-occupations and ideals of their own time: for Virgil's sense of Roman destiny or Milton's project of vindicating the ways of God to man in a great English poem.

But although Milton's poem is in an important sense the *Aeneid* of his age and nation, and vividly projects its loyalty and its debt to its predecessor, it also turns it back on Virgilian (and Homeric) themes, 'the wrauth/Of stern *Achilles* . . . or rage/Of *Turnus* for *Lavinia* disespous'd' (IX. 13 ff.). He even claims that his subject is 'Not less but more Heroic' than these and adds a list of typical epic and romance elements (itself verging on a kind of mock-heroic derision) which he had no wish to emulate, though he had once considered such things: battles, races, games and 'gorgious Knights'. His point here is not the abandonment of a classical for a 'national' theme (though like Dryden he had toyed with the idea of an Arthurian poem), but a radical retreat from the principal subject-matter of the

[13] Watson, II. 292–3. Dryden accused Blackmore of stealing the idea from him. Milton had considered an Arthurian epic before Dryden.

[14] Graham Hough, *The Last Romantics* (London, Methuen, 1961), p. 132.

epic, including many Biblical or Christian epics: 'Warrs, hitherto the onely Argument/Heroic deemd' (IX. 28–9).[15]

Such language, within the poems, puts Milton into an adversary relation with the epic tradition which is in some ways ambiguous as the relation of mock-heroic to the epic was ambiguous. It retains Milton's reverence for the classical models, whose form and structure and whose elevation of style and perspective he 'imitated', while conveying that neither he nor his age was in tune with their ethos. Like Pope and so many others, he was openly disturbed by epic morality, the cruelty and bloodshed and the exaltation of war, and he fell back, as others did, on a partial separation of that morality itself from the larger totality of the great heroic poems in which it is contained.[16]

The successors to Milton whose tribute to epic took the form of mock-heroic poems, but who like Milton had no wish to convey any radically hostile imputation against the epic originals, effected the separation by the method, though not in the manner, which he appeared to propose: by largely avoiding the subject-matter of war. It is seldom remarked that when we speak of mock-heroic, we almost always refer to stylistic or rhetorical parody, and hardly ever to the characteristic subject-matter of epic poems. But the fact reflects a characteristic emphasis in the mock-heroic works themselves. *Mac Flecknoe* and *The Dunciad* leave battles out altogether, though *The Dunciad* has everything else: a Virgilian 'progress', games, hell, prophecy and the rest, while Boileau's *Lutrin*, Garth's *Dispensary* and *The Rape of the Lock* contain mock-battles of a trifling and ludicrously unmilitary or unsanguinary kind. A glance in the Pope Concordance at the words *blood, bleed* and their derivatives reveals virtually no significant instances in either of the mock-heroic poems, but many dozens in the translations of Homer: the *Dunciad*'s action is in this regard epitomized by 'Pomp without guilt, of bloodless swords and maces' (I.87). The only thing approaching Homeric bloodshed in *The Dispensary* occurs in a ridiculed recitation of Blackmore's 'straight' Arthurian pieces, rather than in the main mock-heroic idiom through which the poem articulates its allusions

[15] See also *P.L.*., XI, 689 ff., for scornful comments on the martial values called heroic.
[16] On this, see *Henry Fielding and the Augustan Ideal Under Stress*, pp. 158–9, 168–9 nn.25–6; Pope, Preface to *Iliad* and note to *Iliad* XIII. 471 (TE, VII, li, 14; VIII. 129). See also the comment in *Spectator*, No. 548, 28 November 1712, on Homer's Achilles as 'Morally Vicious, and only Poetically Good'.

to ancient epics and conducts its own narrative business.[17] It is a bookish joke within a bookish joke. It is striking that the mock-battles are frequently 'battles of books', whether in the strictly physical sense in which opponents hurl romances and other volumes at each other in *Le Lutrin* (V. 123–216), or in an allegorized sense even further removed from physical contact, as in Swift's prose *Battle*, where what is spilled is ink or some parody of ichor or 'nectarous' fluid and where (in one of epic's more genial moods) severed bodies 'soon unite again' or are restored or metamorphosed by divine intervention.[18]

The unsanguinary wound has a tiny source in *Iliad*, V. 339–40, where a wounded immortal sheds ichor or (as Byron rhymingly put it, perhaps in mockery of Hobbes's translation of Homer) 'some such other spiritual liquor'.[19] The original Homeric episode, so unlike his gory battle scenes, seems tailor-made for genial mock-heroic imitation, as Swift and Pope and Byron showed, but it is interesting that it is also used in *Paradise Lost*, in a passage which also includes an example of that instant celestial healing in which airy substance soon unites again:

> th'Ethereal substance clos'd
> Not long divisible, and from the gash
> A stream of Nectarous humor issuing flowd
> Sanguin, such as Celestial Spirits may bleed,
> And all his Armour staind erewhile so bright.
>
> (*P.L.*, VI. 330–4)

---

[17] *Dispensary*, 2nd edn, 1699, IV. 178 ff., in *Poems on Affairs of State*, . . . *Volume 6: 1697–1704*, ed. Frank H. Ellis (New Haven, Yale), p. 101.

[18] For the spilling of ink, and divine repair-work, see *Battle of the Books*, in *Prose Writings of Jonathan Swift*, ed. Herbert Davis and others (Oxford, Blackwell, 1939–68), I. 143, 155, 159. For airy substance uniting again, see *Rape of the Lock*, III. 152; for ichor used as divine ink, see *Dunciad*, II. 92.

[19] *Vision of Judgement*, xxv; cf. Hobbes's *Iliads*, 1676, p. 68, where what is shed is not human blood, 'but *Ichor*./For Gods . . ./Have in their Veins another kind of Liquor'. Spence reported Pope as saying that there were several passages from Hobbes's translation which 'if they had been writ on purpose to ridicule that poet, would have done very well', and instancing 'the Ichor' among them (*Observations, Anecdotes*, etc., ed. James M. Osborn (Oxford, Clarendon Press, 1966), No. 451; *Anecdotes*, ed. S.W. Singer (London, W.H. Carpenter, 1820), p. 210; *Observations, Anecdotes*, ed. Edmund Malone (London, John Murray, 1820), p. 285. The two earliest editions of Spence appeared in 1820, the year before Byron's poem was written. Byron was reading Spence early in 1821 (*Letters and Journals*, ed. Leslie A. Marchand (London, John Murray, 1973–81), VIII. 14, 16, 21, 61.

Milton (whom Pope cites in his note to his translation of the
Homeric passage,[20] as well as at *Dunciad*, II. 92, and refers to without
quoting at the corresponding passage in *The Rape of the Lock*) is not
being 'mock-heroic'. The nectarous bleeding of Satan is not genial
but spectacular. The fact that it is Satan who is wounded ensures that
no great distress need be felt at the thought of his suffering, and the
brio of 'Armour staind' has a touch of jeering triumph. Even so a
saving suggestion is created that the wound is not for real in human
terms, as well as healing instantly anyway. This is a central feature of
the War in Heaven whereas the episode of divine bloodshed in
Homer is incidental. Milton rejected the theme of heroic warfare not
by simply bypassing it (in the manner of *The Dunciad*), but by
transferring it wholly from the human to the celestial domain. The
epic's traditional preoccupation with war is preserved on a plane
which escapes the censures of a human morality. War in the disreputable human sense is sublimated as well as 'derealized'. The War
in Heaven is too high to arouse our disapproval of war, much as the
mock-battles of *Le Lutrin* or *The Rape of the Lock* are too low.

Where Milton attacks war outright in the poem, or declares
against the epic view that it is the only argument heroic deemed, he
might be seen as making a more radical critique of the epic tradition
than ever the mock-heroic did. It is perhaps only because he includes
this critique that he was able to achieve success in a 'straight' as
distinct from a *mock*-epic. But the War in Heaven, as the poem's
counterpart of epic wars, is not directly implicated in Milton's
condemnation of secular warfare, and the epic models remain essentially undamaged by this particular imitation of them. The War in
Heaven is righteous as no other war can be, as well as incapable of
killing anyone. There is a degree of separation of the anti-war
morality from the admired epics which are said at one level to offend
against it. Where many other Biblical or Christian epics necessarily
retained the traditional elements of human warfare, Milton overcame the problem partly by placing his celestial war outside the
normal range of criticism, and partly by shifting his main focus
onto non-martial themes traditionally forbidden by epic theorists:
Brower has said well that while Renaissance critics asked for a
Christian colouring which yet excluded the 'central mysteries of the

---

[20] Pope's *Iliad*, V. 422, 424 nn.; cf. Pope's *Iliad*, V. 1009 ff. (Homer, V. 899 ff.)
and note, for an example of quick-healing divine wounds (*TE*, VII. 287–9,
320–1).

faith', Milton boldly 'chose the prohibited subject and wrote the most successful heroic poem of the Renaissance'.[21]

The mock-heroic poems of the next generation generally side-stepped the issue of battle altogether. Pope indeed softened or excised some of the grimmer Homeric cruelties even from his translation of the *Iliad*. Goriness on anything approaching the Homeric scale seems to have been the property of Bartholomew Fair spectacles like Settle's *Siege of Troy*, widely despised as the kind of demotic rubbish where 'Farce and Epic get a jumbled race' (*Dunciad*, I. 70: Settle is prominent in the poem, playing Anchises to Theobald–Cibber's Aeneas).[22] It is as though Pope and the other mock-heroic poets were determined to protect the epic originals from the disrepute which might accrue to them from any serious reminder of bloody deeds.

Swift went further. I have argued elsewhere that this most unremittingly parodic of eighteenth-century writers hardly ever attempted mock-*epic* (though he mocked most other forms of poetic inflation), as though anxious to avoid damaging the originals through any unintended energies of his irony, or contaminating them by exposure to parody, however innocent of anti-epic purposes. *The Battle of the Books*, the only sustained exception, is in prose and offers itself simultaneously as mock-journalese in a way which draws some potential disapproval from the alternative or epic model. It is also only a paper fight. It is notable that whenever Swift attacks war, it is in contexts conspicuously free of epic associations.

Procedures designed to shield the epic from the risks of both moral disapproval and parodic ridicule could take various forms. A late example is the mock-heroic of Fielding's *Jonathan Wild*, which operates at two removes from epic originals. The first remove is effected by Fielding's use of the terms 'heroic' and 'great' to convey certain moral turpitudes as such, and in abstraction from any pressing reminder of the doings of particular epic heroes: the words, so harpingly reiterated, ask to be translated directly into some obvious moral opposite ('wicked', 'murderous', 'thieving'), rather than related to any heroic personage or episode in an epic original. (Similarly, Pope's 'serious' epic on Brutus looks as if it would have

[21] R.A. Brower, *Alexander Pope. The Poetry of Allusion* (London, Oxford University Press, 1968), p. 102.

[22] See *Henry Fielding and the Augustan Ideal Under Stress*, pp. 213, 226nn.; and Pat Rogers, 'Pope, Settle, and The Fall of Troy', *Studies in English Literature*, XV (1975), 447–58.

become a didactic or philosophical poem, largely focused on moral and social questions in abstraction from any typically epic action.) Secondly, where famous 'heroes' are referred to, the book insinuates a distinction between those from 'real life', past (Alexander, Caesar) or present (Walpole), and those from revered heroic poems. The latter seldom appear, and when they do distinctions quickly establish themselves. Fireblood is ironically described as Wild's *fidus Achates*, but the first time this happens Fielding takes care to separate epic from history by adding immediately 'or rather the Hephaestion of our Alexander' (III. iv)[23]. He is thus promptly redefined as the henchman of a historical conqueror whom Fielding despises, rather than the faithful friend of an admired epic hero. Since Fireblood is usually called faithful when he is being pointedly *un*faithful, a two-fold irony comes into being which suggests that he is all too unlike the one, and all too like the other.

A similar ironic doubling or split-level allusiveness, pointedly distinguishing between poetic and historical parallels, underlies the Virgilian 'progress' of *The Dunciad*. The westward removal of Dulness's empire 'from the City to the polite World', Scriblerus tells us, replicates the *Aeneid*'s westward displacement of 'the empire of Troy . . . to Latium'.[24] It also involves comic extensions of the legend that Britain was founded by a further stepping westward, that of Aeneas's descendant Brutus (the subject of Pope's projected late epic), and the consequent idea of London as a new Troy and new Rome. The court and polite world were to the west of the City, and the poem's brooding sense is of unlettered and aldermanic hordes pressing upon it from the easterly regions of trade and Grub Street: a local replay, if Pope but knew it, of a westward drift which has been said to be a recurrent characteristic of the growth of great cities.[25] Set against Aeneas's voyages, it becomes matter for a simple mock-heroic put-down. But another westward movement is also brought into play, that of the invasions of the Roman Empire and 'all the western world' (III.100) by barbarians from the East and North, whose resemblance to the encroachments on Pope's London is a direct rather than a reverse one. As in *Jonathan Wild* a disreputable phenomenon is shown up against both a Virgilian and a 'historical'

---

[23] *Henry Fielding and the Augustan Ideal Under Stress*, pp. 153–4.
[24] 'Martinus Scriblerus of the Poem'. The fullest discussion of this aspect of the poem is Aubrey L. Williams, *Pope's Dunciad. A Study of its Meaning* (London, Methuen, 1955).
[25] Claude Lévi-Strauss, *Tristes Tropiques* (Paris, Plon, 1955), pp. 136–7.

model, the parallels with epic registering an unheroic decline, and those with history a disreputable continuity.

Such separations of fact from artefact were a necessary man-oeuvre, if the idealized reverence for the ancient past was to survive the evidence, abundant in every kind of classical text, that older times were as rich in human depravity as more recent ones. The suggestion that historical precedents are likely to be uglier than epic ones also reflects old assumptions that poetry (and especially heroic poetry) reaches 'above the life' and expresses a higher truth than that of mere phenomena. The famous Aristotelian distinction between the truth of poetry and the truth of history might even, in the hands of some of the lordlier theorists, imply a sarcastic downgrading of the 'histor-ian' to a mere pedlar of facts, or journalist. The mock-epic of *The Battle of the Books* is simultaneously mock-journalese ('A Full and True Account of the Battel Fought last Friday . . .'), and Fielding's scorn of low-grade fact-mongers is well known.[26] Pope's note on Caxton, one of 'The Classics of an Age that heard of none' at *Dunciad*, I. 147 ff., identifies him as 'a Printer [who] . . . translated into prose Virgil's Aeneis, as a history; of which he speaks, in his Proeme, in a very singular manner, as of a book hardly known'. Caxton's trade, his 'rude' old-spelt English (always an easy victim of Augustan mirth) gloatingly reproduced by Pope, his imputed ignorance of humane letters are typical targets of anti-duncic artil-lery. The fact, which had aroused mockery since the early sixteenth century, that he translated Virgil from a French translation, placed him on a par with Welsted, one of Pope's dunces, whose Longinus was described in Swift's *On Poetry: A Rapsody*, l. 261, as 'Translated from *Boileau's* Translation'.[27] But it is Caxton's double degrading of

---

[26] The most recent discussion, whose emphases differ from mine, is Brian McCrea, 'Romances, Newspapers, and the Style of Fielding's True History', *Studies in English Literature*, XXI (1981), 471–80.

[27] On Caxton's Virgil and early attacks on it, see N.F. Blake, *Caxton and his World* (London, Deutsch, 1969), pp. 195–6, 202; C.S. Lewis, *English Literature in the Sixteenth Century* (Oxford, Clarendon Press, 1954), p. 81. Pope evidently had not read Caxton's work, but obtained the text of 'CAXTON's *Preface to his Translation of* VIRGIL' from Lord Oxford in 1728 (*Correspondence*, II. 498), printing it as an Appendix to the editions of 1729 to score a point against Theobald. From 1735, when the Appendix was dropped, Pope quoted from the Preface in his note to the Caxton reference in the poem (TE, V. xxiv n., 79–80, 213–16, 281). Caxton's *Eneydos* (1490) has been published as Early English Text Society Extra Series, No. 57, 1890, rptd 1962.

Virgil, into prose and into *history*, which is of interest to the present argument, because it is evidently represented as an illiterate error and especially as a gross trivializing of Virgil's poem. Caxton, as quoted, speaks praisingly of 'historyes' and 'historye', in a sense which seems to slide between history and story (cf. French *histoire*), as Fielding was often to do with ironic playfulness. It may be part of Pope's point that the *Aeneid* had been degraded not only to mere history, but to false history or 'low' fiction. The business of epic is *high* fiction, and it seemed necessary at this time, though this was not always deliberately acknowledged, to stress the extra-factuality (in the sense of their being somehow outside the factual domain) or superfactuality ('above the life') of epic doings as much as their loftiness as such: Caxton had certainly not altogether overlooked the latter, even in the remarks Pope quotes.

This helps to explain a further feature of Pope's two-way parallel for the dunces' westward progress. Fielding's Fireblood and Wild are the equivalents in viciousness to Hephaestion and Alexander, but they are small-time scoundrels who reduce these ancient historical counterparts, men of imperial scope and power, to their own shoddy level. The process is doubtless assisted by the flattening medium of prose. Their *epic* counterparts, Achates and Aeneas, being opposites rather than direct likenesses, are morally undiminished, though the prose medium and the small-time sleaziness of the *Jonathan Wild* scene may leave them, 'poetically' speaking, somewhat flattened too. This effect is the reverse of what normally happens in *The Dunciad*, where moral reduction and contempt are accompanied by a poetic *aggrandisement*, a sense of grandeur however polluted: 'Great Cibber's brazen, brainless brothers', 'Slow rose a form, in majesty of Mud' (I. 32, II. 326).

A similar majesty, even more richly orchestrated, is conveyed in the famous account of barbarian invasions:

> Soon as they dawn, from Hyperborean skies
> Embody'd dark, what clouds of Vandals rise!
> Lo! where Maeotis sleeps, and hardly flows
> The freezing Tanais thro' a waste of snows,
> The North by myriads pours her mighty sons,
> Great nurse of Goths, of Alans, and of Huns!
> See Alaric's stern port! the martial frame
> Of Genseric! and Attila's dread name!
> See the bold Ostrogoths on Latium fall;
> See the fierce Visigoths on Spain and Gaul . . . (III. 85 ff.)

This leads to cultural catastrophe, but the lights go out with a certain splendour. If the dunces are the modern avatars of these invading hordes, the fact confers on them an importance richly at odds with the contemptible character we know them to have in the 'prose sense' of the poem. And their historical originals, instead of being wholly distinguished from alternative epic models in the manner we have already observed elsewhere, are themselves given some epic associations. The passage derives from Milton:

> A multitude, like which the populous North
> Pourd never from her frozen loins, to pass
> *Rhene* or the *Danaw*, when her barbarous Sons
> Came like a Deluge . . .
>
> (*P.L.*, I. 351 ff.)

a sure sign of highly deliberate elevation in Pope.[28] (In the 'Postscript to the *Odyssey*' Pope suggests that he has made 'some use . . . of the style of *Milton*' in order to 'dignify and solemnize' the 'plainer parts' of Homer himself.)[29]

Johnson reports that the Tanais couplet was the one in all Pope's works by which Pope 'declared his own ear to be most gratified'. He added drily that he could not discover 'the reason of this preference'.[30] But the *fact*, if it is one, is consistent with the bravura of the passage, its almost festive grandeur. Its curious elevation of deplorable events into a species of neo-Miltonic gorgeousness is, in particular, comparable to a striking feature of the much-discussed 'Mob of Metaphors' sequence (I. 55–78), with its topsy-turvy splendours:

> In cold December fragrant chaplets blow,
> And heavy harvests nod beneath the snow.

This is an official rebuke, in the manner of *Peri Bathous*, to Grub Street poetasters who get things wrong.[31] But readers keep finding

---

[28] For other verbal sources of Pope's passage, see TE, V. 156–7 n.

[29] TE, X. 390.

[30] *Lives of the English Poets*, ed. G. Birkbeck Hill (Oxford, Clarendon Press, 1905), III. 250.

[31] E.g. *Art of Sinking in Poetry*, pp. 48–9, including an instance involving Blackmore, and pp. 19–24, several cases of 'this happy and antinatural way of thinking'. See the good discussion by Howard Erskine-Hill, *Pope: The Dunciad* (London, Arnold, 1972), pp. 28–31.

in such passages a 'surrealist' loveliness of a kind which (like his pleasure in the Tanais lines) might suggest a more direct imaginative surrender on the poet's part to the beauty he creates out of rejected ugliness.

Pope was assisted in this by the fact that the images he scorned in one sense as 'Figures ill pair'd, and Similies unlike' could be indulged in another as legitimate instances of the figure *adynaton*, 'impossibility', in its commonest 'world upside down' form ('Realms shift their place, and Ocean turns to land'), practised since ancient times in certain rhetorical situations by Theocritus, Virgil, Horace, Ovid and many others. (Indeed Pope had Horace's own precedent for condemning such muddles in critical precept, mimicking their extravagance, and using them straight.)[32] In Pope's December chaplets and snow-clad harvests, an unacknowledged loveliness, superficially at odds with the ostensible argument, is thus reintegrated into a mainstream of classically sanctioned poetical 'beauties',[33] as the passage about the barbarian hordes is unexpectedly naturalized into a tradition of epic grandeur by means of its Miltonic mimicry. Whenever, as with the hordes, the ugliness so insolently transfigured tends specifically towards heroic rather than Horatian or Ovidian models, a feeling arises that *The Dunciad*, as the last of the great mock-heroic poems, is close to turning back into some form of epic in its own right; much as *Paradise Lost*, the last of the classical epics, occasionally seemed poised on the edge of mock-heroic.[34]

---

[32] See the important recent discussion of these lines and the *adynaton*-tradition by A.D. Nuttall, 'Fishes in the Trees', *Essays in Criticism*, XXIV (1974), 20–38, esp. 27 ff. For reference to studies and lists of *adynata*, see my note 'Rabelais and Horace: A Contact in *Tiers Livre*, ch. III', *French Studies*, XIX (1965), 376–8 and nn. 8–12.

[33] There are also some Shakespearean precedents for specific elements in Pope's couplet: 'At Christmas I no more desire a rose/Than wish a snow in May's new fangled shows' (*LLL*, I. i. 105–6); 'hoary-headed frosts/Fall in the fresh lap of the crimson rose;/And on old Hiems' thin and icy crown,/An odorous chaplet of sweet summer buds/Is, as in mockery, set' (*MND*, II. i. 107–11).

[34] See above, pp. 49 ff. For an effect of contemptuous comedy in *Paradise Lost*, itself verging on mock-heroic and drawn up on by Pope in the Dunciadic games, see II. 947 ff.: 'So eagerly the Fiend/O'er bog or steep, through strait, rough, dense or rare,/With head, hands, wings or feet persues his way,/And swims or sinks, or wades, or creeps, or flies.' Pope imitated and cited these lines at *Dunciad*, II. 63 ff.

This tends in *The Dunciad* against that separation between epic and history which I have been discussing, but it does so by casting an epic grace over squalid doings rather than by an opposite effect sometimes found in *Jonathan Wild*. It also differs conspicuously from the great modern counterpart of Pope's passage, the lines about 'hooded hordes swarming/Over endless plains, stumbling in cracked earth', in *The Waste Land* (ll. 368 ff.). There is a technical difference, which is perhaps only a matter of local emphasis. Pope's hordes are in the historical past, but bear on the present, Eliot's belong to the present but are linked to all the crumbling civilizations of the past,

> Falling towers
> Jerusalem Athens Alexandria
> Vienna London
> Unreal

In both cases past and present reflect ill on one another, and we should remember that *The Waste Land* has a Popeian ancestry. It began life containing satiral couplets modelled on *The Rape of the Lock*, with a Swiftian admixture. Its method of playing off a decaying present against an ambiguously noble past derives partly from Augustan techniques of ironic literary allusion; and it shares with *The Dunciad* especially its great theme of cultural disintegration.

But the passing in view of history's fallen empires in Eliot's lines is dry, fragmented, pinched: a bare list, its ancient splendours picked clean, as it were, by the passage of time and successions of hooded hordes. There is nothing of the blowsy amplitude of Pope's invading barbarians, also relentlessly defeating each successive portion of the civilized world, but doing so with a steady conquering march which belies the disintegration, a gaudy stateliness which holds the broken pieces together in its single onward sweep. The destruction itself is apprehended with a nobility and a coherence which derive largely from Pope's ability to measure it against the normative background of an epic tradition still majestic and stable enough to provide a kind of ordering focus even to the vision of disaster. The order is experienced not conceptually (for at that level it is mainly a disappointed aspiration) but stylistically, in that special feeling evoked throughout the poem's vast network of allusion that the heroic imagination from Homer to Milton is a single continuously flowering thing. It is, ironically, and in a more restricted sense than Eliot intended, that very 'tradition' which Eliot described as a 'feeling that the whole of the literature of Europe from Homer . . . has a simultaneous existence and composes a simultaneous order', and the absence of which *The Waste Land*, with its frenetic, dislocated and eclectic allusiveness, so poignantly registers. 'The existing monuments form an ideal order among themselves', but what their presence in the poem reveals is the 'heap of broken images . . . fragments . . . shored against my ruins'.[35]

The terms of Eliot's discourse are different from mine and his argument is that each 'really new' work of art modifies and rearranges the tradition. This would properly presuppose that in *The Waste Land* the 'fragments' *are* the 'order'. But the sense in which this is eloquently true does not remove the vivid difference between *The Waste Land* and Pope's presentations of the fragmented, the chaotic, the 'uncreating'. Pope's poem is full of embryos and abortions, images unfinished or twisted or broken-backed. They are, however, contained within the larger visible stabilities of the Popeian universe, and sometimes display their own miniature order: 'Maggots half-form'd in rhyme exactly meet' (l. 61). The line occurs in the sequence which includes the *adynata*, and like them is caught in some odd self-vitalizing circularities. The perverse 'anti-order' of maggots rhyming 'exactly' is noted as a poor parody of good rhyming verse. But it is parodied in reverse, or 'upwards', in a poem which not only mimics such things, but itself also 'in rhyme exactly meets' in its own *full*-formed state.

Pope's own triumphant command of couplet-styles, even as he plays at bad couplets, is part of that bravura expression of normative harmonies and coherences which distinguishes his mock-heroic from Eliot's. Eliot too attempted couplets in 'The Fire Sermon', until Pound told him to remove them because 'you cannot parody Pope unless you can write better verse than Pope'.[36] These miniature coherences, like the larger ones, were it seems not for him, even at that doubly protective distance of *mock*-mock-heroic which his

[35] 'Tradition and the Individual Talent', *Selected Essays* (London, Faber, 1953), pp. 14, 15; *Waste Land*, ll. 22, 430. For other recent discussions of *The Dunciad* and *The Waste Land*, see Patricia Meyer Spacks, *An Argument of Images* (Cambridge, Mass., Harvard, 1971), pp. 96–104, 125–32; J.S. Cunningham, 'Pope, Eliot, and "The Mind of Europe" ', in *The Waste Land in Different Voices*, ed. A.D. Moody (London, Arnold, 1974), pp. 67–85.

[36] *The Waste Land. A Facsimile and Transcript of the Original Drafts*, ed. Valerie Eliot (London, Faber, 1971), p. 127 n., cited from Eliot's Introduction to Pound's *Selected Poems* (London, Faber, 1948), p. 18.

'imitation' of *The Rape of the Lock* had set out to be. For a mock-heroic in couplets in Eliot's time, we have to look to Roy Campbell, roughly the Blackmore of the day. Traditional mock-heroic was as impossible in Eliot's day as the straight epic had become in Pope's. As Pope could not complete his epic, but wrote a *Dunciad*, Eliot did not complete his mock-heroic, but achieved *The Waste Land*, while the Blackmores who once wrote *King Arthur*s were now turning their hand to 'satirical' *Georgiad*s.

The scrambling of parallel and contrast in both *The Dunciad* and *The Waste Land* is a version of that 'perception, not only of the pastness of the past, but of its presence' of which Eliot wrote in 'Tradition and the Individual Talent'.[37] Eliot's own poem provides an essentially negative model for this. It offers a much more insecure assertion that ancient grandeurs were as noble as a mock-heroic insistence on later decay might make them out to be, and sees them indeed as containing the germ of present sickness. Indeed its effect, much more than we ever feel in Pope's poem, is to show the past as contaminated by the present: a negative version, in some ways, of Eliot's sense of the way 'tradition' and its past triumphs may be retroactively modified and enriched by the new. Pope was as un-likely to give voice to such a 'modern' presumption as to the negative obverse. The nearest he comes to it is a protest at the undervaluing of the best living poets, which is anyway Horatian in origin and has an ancient '*Precedent* to plead': the undervaluation is itself ironically conceived in Pope's or Swift's eyes as a paradoxical form of perennial 'modernism'. And it was easier for Pope than for Eliot to suspend scepticism of heroic models. He could retain suffi-cient confidence in their validity to feel that the modern failure to match their standard was culpable or contemptible. Eliot proposed something like the same decline from high to low, but he could only sustain the comparison by extending his scepticism to the past, conferring upon it some of his contempt for the present as Pope conferred on the contemptible present a residual sense of heroic value from the past.

That value was of course notional, indirect and 'fictive'. It rested on heroic poems rather than heroic deeds, and the separation in Pope's *Dunciad* between the grandeurs of ancient utterance and the doings of historical villains, like the sheer omission from it of the chief epic subject-matter of carnage and war, emphasizes this in a

---

[37] *Selected Essays*, p. 14.

way in which Eliot's poem does not. Eliot's poem (whose allusions to earlier grandeurs are no longer 'epic' in any strict or dominant sense anyway) tends persistently to collapse that distinction between past facts and past artefacts which provided some Augustan poets with an unspoken saving clause. The meannesses and depravities of the present are continually referred back to painful precedents both in poems and in life, in Ovid or Webster as well as in the historical lives of Elizabeth and Leicester.

In this, as I suggested elsewhere, *The Waste Land* finds a rudimentary Augustan predecessor not in *The Dunciad* but in *Jonathan Wild*, in occasional passages which breach the work's usual attempt to insulate epic precedents from the discredit which can freely be lavished on Alexander and Caesar.[38] Thus the schoolboy Wild was not only 'a passionate admirer of heroes, particularly of Alexander the Great', but (though unwilling 'to acquire a competent sufficiency in the learned languages') also expressed a high regard for certain episodes in both *Iliad* and *Aeneid*, as he heard them translated at school. For example, 'He was wonderfully pleased with that passage in the eleventh Iliad where Achilles is said to have bound two sons of Priam upon a mountain, and afterwards to have released them for a sum of money. This was, he said, alone sufficient to refute those who affected a contempt for the wisdom of the ancients' (I.iii). It is a small effect, easily discountable, up to a point, by its comic context of schoolboy oafishness, and by the character of the speaker: Wild is no more an authority on 'the wisdom of the ancients' than Martinus Scriblerus was on the status of epic poems as 'the greatest Work Human Nature is capable of'.

But an ambiguous complication of the mock-heroic contrast nevertheless makes itself felt, implying on the one hand that the heroic norm is better or nobler than the modern reality, but suggesting at the same time that there may not have been much to choose between them after all. The absurd tendentiousness of Wild's conception of Homeric epic connects uneasily with the common recognition that Homeric times were, as Pope himself put it, an age of 'Rapine and Robbery',[39] and that this was reflected in the poems, though distinguishable from their total greatness as imaginative achievements. It is consistent with the hope, which had been recently

[38] *Henry Fielding and the Augustan Ideal Under Stress*, pp. 156–8.
[39] Preface to *Iliad*, TE, VII. 14.

expressed in Thomas Blackwell's *Enquiry into the Life and Writings of Homer* (1735), '*That we may never be a proper Subject of an* Heroic Poem', which in turn goes back to a line of thinking most memorably formulated by Cowley in 1656: 'a warlike, various, and a tragical age is best to *write of*, but worst to *write in*.'[40] If such constatations, as we have seen throughout, left enough imaginative leeway for a deep and flourishing devotion to what Fielding, in a famous passage at the end of his life, referred to as 'those noble poems that have so justly collected the praise of all ages', it should be remembered that these very words occur in a strange late act of revisionism: 'I must confess I should have honoured and loved Homer more had he written a true history of his own times in humble prose.'[41]

Jonathan Wild's schoolboy celebration of the gangster-virtues of Homeric and Virgilian heroes is a version of an old connection, made especially familiar in our time in several formulations by Auden and Isherwood, between the ethics of heroes, gangsters and schoolboy toughs.[42] If it has, in the case of Wild, a certain backhanded geniality, this geniality is of a rather different order from that of the epic 'games' in Book II of *The Dunciad*, with their races and their 'urinating, tickling, shouting, and diving competitions', about whose childlike character Emrys Jones has written tellingly.[43]

In both the poem and the novel, an almost affectionate humour is allowed to compete occasionally with the serious business of scorning dangerous enemies. But where the schoolboy antics of the dunces exist in a holiday mood of gleeful irresponsible play, Wild's schoolboy enthusiasms, like his occasional displays of adult childishness, are all concerned with joyless projects of plunder and bullying. If a soft spot is nevertheless to be entertained for Wild, contrary to some conventional or 'face-value' readings of him as a figure of dark unrelieved diabolism, it is because of his boorish effrontery, the

---

[40] Blackwell, p. 28; Cowley, *Poems*, ed. A.R. Waller (Cambridge, Cambridge University Press, 1905), p. 7. It is in this same Preface of 1656 that Cowley discusses his failure to complete his two epics, *The Civil War* and the *Davideis* (pp. 9, 11–12).

[41] Preface to *Journal of a Voyage to Lisbon*, ed. Harold E. Pagliaro (New York, Nardon Press, 1963), p. 26.

[42] On Auden and Isherwood, and schoolboy analogies, see *Henry Fielding and the Augustan Ideal Under Stress*, pp. 172 ff.

[43] 'Pope and Dulness', *Proceedings of the British Academy*, LIV (1968), 253–4.

hapless automatism of his thieving instinct, the clownish failure of his projects. Of playground innocence, of carefree bustle and happy noises and cheerful smut, there is no trace.

Fielding's sympathies were in many ways more relaxed and easy-going than Pope's. But he was readier to see a sinister connection between the childish forms of supposedly harmless mirth or 'practical Jests', and the 'little jocose Mischiefs' of Roman emperors and other tormentors of mankind: Domitian torturing flies, Phalaris and his bull, or (for an epic-related example) Nero, whose 'comical Humours' doubtless included his singing the 'Sack of Ilium' while Rome burned.[44] For Fielding, the link between schoolboy viciousness and murderous tyranny was as immediate as it is in Jarry's Ubu or Alan Coren's Amin: as 'comical' and as brutally horrifying.

When by contrast Pope speaks of 'Domitian . . . killing flies' (*Dunciad*, I. 15 n), it is not in order to imply that this activity, though apparently trivial, leads to more dreadful things; but on the contrary that he the poet, in satirizing dunces, is doing much more than 'killing flies'. The larger-scale cruelties of Domitian are evidently viewed (if viewed at all) with some detachment: Pope leaves them unmentioned, much as epic carnage is left out of view in the body of the poem. This is all the more striking because Pope's argument is that his own attack on the apparently trivial is really concerned with a bigger menace, so that the example of Domitian might have provided an analogy rather than a contrast. Dulness, he says, is

> not to be taken contractedly for mere Stupidity, but in the enlarged sense of the word, for all Slowness of Apprehension, Shortness of Sight, or imperfect Sense of things. It includes . . . Labour, Industry, and some degree of Activity and Boldness: a ruling principle not inert, but turning topsy-turvy the Understanding, and inducing an Anarchy or confused State of Mind.

The point of this 'Bentleian' note is the same as that of Scriblerus's reminder at III.333 of 'what the Dutch stories somewhere relate, that a great part of their Provinces was once overflowed, by a small opening made in one of their dykes by a single *Water-Rat*'.

The point is made here with a certain Swiftian urgency, perhaps

---

[44] See *Henry Fielding and the Augustan Ideal Under Stress*, pp. 192–3, 220–1 nn.

for once outdoing Swift in shocking formulation (cf. Swift's sermon on 'Doing Good': 'The weakest hand can open a floodgate to drown a country, which a thousand of the strongest cannot stop').[45] *The Duncias*'s theme of engulfing disorder is pressingly apprehended, and the sense of a total cultural black-out proceeding from small origins is everywhere apparent. But it is conveyed in images of 'Universal Darkness' and a large sleepiness, not with strongly particularized scenes of disruption and certainly without sanguinary elements. The very convulsions are stately, and from the style which creates such effects it is possible to derive a feeling of reassurance and even stability which we do not find in *Jonathan Wild*, even if we read that work (as I think we should) as a milder or more genial satire than it is often taken to be.

Pope separates the sinister aspects of his theme from the playful ones more completely than Fielding does. For all its menacing features, 'gentle Dulness ever loves a joke' (II.34), and unlike the merry pranks of Jonathan Wild the 'games' in Book II, with all their allegorical imputations of filth and foolishness, attain 'a mock solemnity that is too deeply humorous to be finally cruel'. '*The Dunciad*', Wilson Knight has said, 'is Pope's *Inferno*, his *Macbeth*. That it refuses any violent evil is characteristic, for he writes from a mental horizon where such depths are not of primary importance: he feels . . . "letters" taking the place of "lances" . . .'[46] *The Dunciad* begins, in its first version, by signposting precisely that shift from lances to letters, from 'Arms, and the Man' to 'Books and the Man I sing'. When he later changed this to 'The Mighty Mother, and her Son', it was not in order to return to epic lances, but in some ways to move the poem another step away from epic's ancient matter.[47]

---

[45] *Prose Writings*, IX. 235.

[46] G. Wilson Knight, *The Poetry of Pope, Laureate of Peace* (London, Routledge, 1965), pp. 60, 62. The phrase about letters and lances is from Lyly's *Campaspe*, I. i. 82: Alexander is speaking to Hephaestion.

[47] The opening words respectively of Dryden's translation of the *Aeneid* (*arma virumque cano*), and of the A and B texts of *The Dunciad*. On *The Dunciad* as a poem tending away from the epic tradition, see John E. Sitter, *The Poetry of Pope's Dunciad* (Minneapolis, University of Minnesota Press, 1971).

Blake: The Poet as Prophet

KATHLEEN RAINE

I

Blake is unique in English literature—indeed in English history—for he called himself a prophet. To him his writings and his paintings alike were means, not ends in themselves—the language of his inspired message to the English nation. And he held that all imaginative poets are prophets in the very nature of their inspiration. 'Inspired' poetry differs not in degree but in kind from what Blake calls the 'distinct' and inferior' art which he calls 'Fable or Allegory':

> Fable or Allegory is Form'd by the daughters of Memory. Imagination is surrounded by the daughters of Inspiration . . . Allegory & Vision (del. Visions of the Imagination) ought to be known as Two Distinct Things, & so call'd for the Sake of Eternal Life[1]

—for the sake of eternal life because whereas memory relates only to knowledge received through the senses (natural life) imagination draws its images from inner worlds, from the *mundus imaginalis* and is therefore the self-knowledge of the human spirit itself.

The prophet is by definition one who 'speaks for God' to a tribe or nation. He speaks to a collective conscience and consciousness, and from that transpersonal mind (called by whatever name) of which he is the messenger. The prophet's role is not at all the same as that of the Bard or Ollave of traditional Celtic or Nordic societies, whose office (also a public one) was to celebrate and record notable events of this world. The Bard was the creator and custodian of oral tradition, transmitting the records of the past and praising his own king and warrior heroes of the tribe—or dispraising them: for the Bard was the arbiter of what was worthy to be remembered, combining the roles of journalist and historian, feared and flattered by rulers who were afraid of receiving a bad press. Bardic poetry must

---

[1] *Notebook* p. 68, ed. Geoffrey Keynes (hereafter K.), 604–5.

have been heart-stirring, sung at kings' feasts as the wine-cup went round the board, inspiring companions-in-arms with a sense of glory, loyalty and tribal identity.

The role of the prophet, no less ancient, no less essential to the tribe, was less popular among rulers and heroes; for the prophet neither flattered nor celebrated popular heroes but (in the words of that later seer the Irish poet and painter AE—George Russell) passed on the 'politics of time' the judgment of the 'politics of eternity'. Prophets throughout history have seldom brought the news kings like to hear, have often been persecuted, disbelieved, driven away, regarded as mad; Blake himself being no exception. Yet prophets have been hard to silence, however unwelcome their messages from inner worlds; and indeed the role of shaman and sibyl has been held in honour in those societies who deemed it necessary to consider the inner causes and consequences of events. If the Bard was a recorder of events already enacted, the sibyl, shaman or prophet was consulted on the undertaking of future actions. We know from the story of Balaam that the prophets themselves sometimes were reluctant to deliver unwelcome judgments, for the inner and the outer aspect of things may be very different; and Troy always prefers not to believe god-inspired Cassandra.

Thus prophecy was not traditionally associated with poetry or the role of the poet; but Blake uses the terms bard and prophet interchangeably. His bards are prophets, inspired messengers of the inner and higher worlds.

> Hear the Voice of the Bard!
> Who Present Past & Future sees;
> Whose ears have heard
> The Holy Word
> That walk'd among the ancient trees,
> Calling the lapsed Soul
> And weeping in the evening dew . . .
> (*Songs of Innocence*, 'The Voice of the Ancient Bard.' K. 126)

The Bard 'calls' to the fallen souls of humankind banished from among the 'ancient trees' of Paradise. The voice of the Bard is the voice of God heard by Adam in Eden before the Fall, the onset of the night of spiritual forgetfulness. For Blake Milton is the type of the inspired poet, and in the poem that bears his name he is called 'the awakener' and also the Bard. The theme of Blake's *Milton* is poetic

inspiration. The 'immortal/Loud voic'd Bard' is challenged to declare the source of his 'high toned Song':

> . . .'If it is true, if the acts have been perform'd,
> 'Let the Bard himself witness. Where hadst thou this terrible
> song?'
> The Bard replied: 'I am Inspired: I know it is Truth! for I sing
> 'According to the inspiration of the Poetic Genius,
> 'Who is the eternal all-protecting Divine Humanity.'
> (*Milton*, p. 13, l. 46, K.495)

Blake was of course taking his unhistorical view of the function of
the Bard from the picturesque conception of ancient British society
current in his day; but his view of prophetic inspiration was his own
and in no sense romantic or archaeological. It concerned above all his
own ever-present sense of vocation:

> . . . I rest not from my great task:
> To open the Eternal Worlds, to open the immortal Eyes
> Of Man inwards into the Worlds of thought, into Eternity
> Ever expanding in the Bosom of God, the Human Imagination.
> (*Jerusalem*, Pl.5, K. 623)

   The prophet in voicing events of these inner worlds is by no means
recording 'subjective' experience. It has been assumed in every
primitive society that the entranced shaman or sibyl is in communi-
cation with an order of inner realities which are objective to the
empirical ego of the individual. The real world, the *mundus imaginalis*, Henry Corbin, in his distinguished works on Iranian mystical
philosophy, has given the name 'imaginal' to distinguish it from the
'imaginary' in the sense of make-believe. It is the real world in which
events of the psyche 'take place'; though its places are places of the
mind and not of the physical world. Blake, in the same sense, used
the word Imagination. It is the world of the archetypes of which all
Platonic philosophers (and this term embraces the Sufis no less than
the European Platonists, amongst whom Blake himself must be
numbered) declare:

> There Exist in that Eternal World the Permanent Realities of
> Every Thing which we see reflected in this Vegetable Glass of
> Nature. All Things are comprehended in their Eternal Forms in

the divine body of the Saviour, the True Vine of Eternity, The Human Imagination.[2]

Blake often uses terms which in other contexts might seem to belong to naïve evangelical piety, but which in his usage contain exact and profound psychological or metaphysical meaning; as here 'the Saviour' is said to be the human Imagination, which 'saves' the realities of all things from the mutability and mortality of the world of nature. His time and place did not possess a current language for the discussion of what Coleridge has called 'facts of mind'. Blake regretted that in his own society, whose thought was already coloured by the materialist view of the universe still current today, the inner worlds were so little known:

> The Nature of Visionary Fancy, or Imagination, is very little Known, & the Eternal nature & permanence of its ever Existent Images is consider'd as less permanent than the things of Veget-ative & Generative Nature; yet the Oak dies as well as the Lettuce, but Its Eternal Image & Individuality never dies, but renews by its seed; just so the Imaginative Image returns by the seed of Con-templative Thought; the Writings of the Prophets illustrate these conceptions of the Visionary Fancy by their various sublime & Divine Images seen in the World of Vision.[3]

A change has come in this century with the reopening of the inner worlds in terms of the psychological studies of Freud and Jung, and with the translation and dissemination of Indian and Far-Eastern philosophy. The mystical theology of the Sufis is perhaps closest to that of Blake; and in the translations and commentaries of that great sage and scholar Henry Corbin many parallels are to be found. Corbin expounds the doctrine of Sohravardi in which the meta-physics of the Imagination is inseparable from the ontology of the *mundus imaginalis*, the intermediary between the intellectual world of pure intelligences and the world of sense perception. The 'active Imagination' can be angel or demon:

> Tantôt livrée aux séductions de l'estimative, elle est la proie des perceptions sensibles recueillies dans le *sensorium* et ne secrète que l'imaginaire. Tantôt au service de l'intellect, elle est alors l'Imagination intellective ou cogitative, et elle est l'organe de pénétration dans le monde intermédiaire qui est le monde *imagi-*

---

[2] *Notebook* pp. 69–70, K. 605.   [3] *Notebook*, pp. 68–9, K. 605.

nal, où le spirituel prend subtilement corps (un corps spirituel) et où le corporel se spiritualise. Ce sont les 'images métaphysiques' qu'elle projette alors dans le *sensorium*. De la compréhension de cette doctrine dépendra la compréhension que l'on aura, ou non, de la scénographie réelle, du 'réalisme symbolique', des récits mystiques.[4]

(At one time abandoned to the seductions of the estimative faculty, it is at the mercy of sense-perceptions collected in the *sensorium* and only secretes the 'imaginary'; but at other times it is in the service of intellect, and is then the intellective or reflective Imagination, the organ by which we penetrate that intermediate world which is the world of the *imaginal*, wherein the spiritual is subtly embodied (with a spiritual body) and where the corporeal is spiritualized. These are 'metaphysical images' which are then projected into the *sensorium*. Upon the comprehension of this doctrine depends the comprehension (or failure to comprehend) of the real scenography, the 'symbolic realism', of mystical narratives.)

No poet knew better than Blake this imaginal world where ideas are experienced as images, and images as meaning:

If the Spectator could Enter into these Images in his Imagination, approaching them on the Fiery Chariot of his Contemplative Thought . . . or could make a Friend & Companion of one of these Images of wonder, which always intreats him to leave mortal things (as he must know), then he would arise from his Grave, then he would meet the Lord in the Air & then he would be happy.[5]

Blake's Lord is the Imagination; Sohravardi's Archangel of the Holy Spirit, the 'shayk' who instructs the seeker in the inner worlds. Such knowledge (so it is believed by all traditions in which the imaginal is described) is not of a 'subjective' order but of an ontological spiritual universe common to all. Blake writes of his painting of the Vision of the Last Judgment that '. . . its Vision is seen by the Imaginative Eye of Every one according to the situation he holds' and that 'to different People it appears differently, as everything else does'.[6]

It is not surprising that in Blake's lifetime the imaginal world was 'very little known' since the prevalent view at that time (expressed

---

[4] *L'Archange Empourpré* (Paris 1976), p. 96.
[5] *Notebook* pp. 82–4, K. 611.   [6] *Notebook* pp. 70, 68–9, K. 604 & 605.

especially by Locke, father of Behaviourist psychology) was that the
senses are the only sources of knowledge and the mind a passive
recipient of information from a lifeless and external universe.
Against this view Blake fought his lifelong battle, never ceasing
to affirm the creative power of mind itself. For Blake, as for the
Hermetica, as for that whole tradition which takes as its ground not
matter but mind itself, the mental universe is experienced and conceived as a Person, called by Blake the 'divine body' in every man, at
once the containing mind and the universe of images it contains.
Other of the Romantic poets were already moving towards the same
conception—Coleridge defined the 'primary Imagination' as 'the
adorable I AM'; and whereas Blake named this Person of the Imagination 'Jesus', Keats, who rejected Christianity, nevertheless wrote in
one of his letters of the same archetypal universe as 'Adam's dream':

> . . . the Imagination may be compared to Adam's dream—he
> awoke and found it truth.

He goes on to affirm

> that Imagination and its empyreal reflection is the same as human
> Life and its Spiritual repetition.[7]

The prototype, Keats declares, 'must be hereafter'. Yet facts of mind
were not to be seriously studied until our own century, and only
now is Blake's prophetic voice beginning to be heard within the
context of a newly rediscovered psychological and metaphysical
dimension.

II

Coleridge was a profound scholar, familiar with the Platonic and
Neoplatonic writings and also with Kant and the German school.
Blake knew the Platonists also, through the English translations
of his acquaintance Thomas Taylor the Platonist. But on Blake's
thought there was one influence of the greatest significance which,
because it lies outside the fields alike of literature and of philosophy
(as these are understood in reputable academic circles) has been
virtually disregarded—the influence of Swedenborg. (Henry
Corbin, be it said, held Swedenborg to be of the greatest significance;

---

[7] *Letters*, No. 31, p. 68.

'the Buddha of the West' as he once described him.) Because in an early work (*The Marriage of Heaven and Hell*) Blake satirized and criticized Swedenborg most of Blake's commentators have prematurely concluded that he early abandoned his Swedenborgian studies, and his immense and continuing influence on Blake has never been given its due weight. Blake was eclectic, certainly; but I would go so far as to say that the basic structure of his system is the Swedenborgian doctrine of the 'Church of the New Jerusalem'. If he satirized Swedenborg in 1790 he nevertheless wrote some thirty years later a poem—*The Everlasting Gospel*—which is virtually a summary of the so-called 'leading doctrines' of the New Church. His very name for the Imagination, 'the Divine Humanity' or 'Divine Body', is Swedenborg's; for whom 'the Lord' or 'Grand Man of the heavens' (so he names the collective Person of the 'heavens' or inner worlds) is made up of the multitudes of human souls which together make up the 'body' of the universal 'Divine Humanity'. The 'innumerable multitudes of eternity' of whom Blake so eloquently writes, appeared to Swedenborg, in the inner worlds, as one man; as they did to Blake himself:

> Then those in Great Eternity met in the Council of God
> As one Man, for contracting their Exalted Senses
> They behold Multitude, or Expanding they behold as one,
> As One Man all the Universal family; & that One Man
> They call Jesus the Christ, & they in him & he in them
> Live in Perfect harmony, in Eden the land of life,
> Consulting as One Man above the Mountain of Snowdon
>   Sublime.
>   (*The Four Zoas*, Night the First, p. 269, K. 277)

To transpose his terms, 'Great Eternity' is the *mundus imaginalis*, humanity's inner universe; the 'exalted senses' are the faculties of the soul which 'contracting' leave only natural perception, but which can expand into the inner and higher worlds—as described also by Corbin in the passage cited above. The One Man is Swedenborg's 'Grand Man of the Heavens' who is the *anthropos* made in the image of God, as described in the first chapter of Genesis; 'Eden, the land of life' is mankind's inner universe and true native country from which we are banished into an externalized nature of 'the Time & Space fixed by the Corporeal Vegetative Eye'.[8] The Holy Mountain is, as

---

[8] *Notebook* pp. 91–2, K. 614.

in other mythologies (Gilead, in Biblical terms, but for Blake Britain's holy mountain, 'Snowdon Sublime'), the summit of spiritual consciousness and dwelling-place of the gods; and the One Man is the single life in which all human experience is contained and bodied forth; the *mundus imaginalis* conceived, as by Swedenborg, as a single living being.

According to Swedenborg every event that occurs in history is conceived first in 'the heavens' or inner worlds. The events of this world are the continuous realization and 'correspondence' of what has first been imagined. In 1757, so Swedenborg taught, a new age or, in his own terms, a new 'Church' came into being in 'the heavens' whose realization in historic terms would follow. This prophecy Blake may have adopted with the more enthusiasm because he was himself born in the year of Swedenborg's prophecy. He felt himself to be the prophet of that New Age, identified himself with it and set himself to discover the nature of this revolution in human consciousness and to dedicate himself to its proclamation and realization. Swedenborg himself stands within a tradition of Millennial prophets, who have perhaps each in their day discerned some inner process at work behind the changes of history, which I hesitate to call 'evolutionary' because the word implies a natural—so to say horizontal—causality which the prophets deny, affirming always a vertical dimension. In Blake's words

> . . . every natural effect has a spiritual cause, and not a natural. Natural cause only seems . . .

In Blake's view, as in Swedenborg's, the causes of historic events are neither economic nor political, but originate in the human Imagination. In his mythological account of history it is Los, the time-spirit who, looking always to the originals which are in eternity, creates the 'moving images' of the time-world of which Plato wrote. According to our imaginings, so is the world continually built and destroyed, as the mills and factories of the Industrial Revolution are themselves images of the 'dark Satanic mills' of the Newtonian universe, that mechanized and externalized universe against which Blake fought his lifelong intellectual war. In the same way he saw in the ideologies of Voltaire and Rousseau the true causes of the French Revolution. In our own lifetime C.G. Jung has pointed out that our atom-bombs are not made by 'science' but by that very dangerous and real being, the human psyche and its imaginings. 'The world hangs by a thin thread, and that thread is the psyche of man,' Jung said in a filmed interview; 'There is no such thing in nature as an H-bomb—that is all man's doing. *We* are the great danger. The psyche is the great danger.' Man's fantasies are real and dangerous, Jung insists.[9] If we live in apocryphal times their terrors are of our own creation and originate in those inner worlds we can no longer regard as unreal or innocuous.

III

Los continually builds and continually destroys the 'Spiritual Fourfold/London, continually building & continually decaying desolate'[10] and Blake conceived the time-spirit as horrified at what he must build in obedience to the fantasies of mankind: 'In fears/He builded it, in rage & in fury.'

Those poems Blake calls 'Prophecies' are the poet's scannings of the inner worlds and the events there enacted; the events of history as these take form in the 'heavens'—and in the hells—of the inner universe of the collective national being. So understood, prophecies are not the scanning of the future, of a fate predetermined in the nature of a mechanized universe; for Imagination is living, creative, for ever renewing itself, changing its theme perpetually in response to experience. We are the agents, not the victims of fate. The prophet who reads those inner events can hope—as Blake certainly hoped —not only to foretell but to change the course of history.

> Prophets in the modern sense of the word have never existed (he wrote). Jonah was no prophet in the modern sense, for his prophecy of Nineveh failed. Every honest man is a Prophet; he utters his opinion both on private & public matters. Thus: If you go on So, the result is So. He never says, such a thing shall happen let you do what you will. A Prophet is a Seer, not an Arbitrary Dictator. It is man's fault if God is not able to do him good, for he gives to the just and to the unjust, but the unjust reject his gift.[11]

However, prophets' success in terms of heeded warnings is not great; nor in this respect was Blake an exception, though, unlike Jonah, he would have rejoiced had his diagnosis of 'the sickness of Albion' been accepted and his salutary advice followed.

[9] *C.G. Jung Speaking* (Princeton 1977), p. 303.
[10] *Jerusalem*, Pl. 53, K. 684.
[11] Annotation to Watson's *Apology*, p. 14, K. 392.

IV

The so-called 'Lambeth Books' entitled 'prophecies' and written in the troubled years of the 1790s are unprecedented in English literature. Blake's detailed allusions to the persons and events of American and French history make it clear that the poet followed these events with passionate concern and exact attention. *The French Revolution: A Poem in Seven Books* makes hard reading for whoever has not a detailed knowledge of the ebb and flow of the events of those years. Only the first book survives; this had already been printed when the mounting tension between England and France persuaded Blake's friend the publisher, Johnson, sympathizer as he was with the cause of the Revolution, that publication would be too dangerous. The loss of the remaining six books is no great disaster, for a single sample of this turbid, turgid work is more than enough. Yet as an attempt to read the events of history from within it is remarkable. To call this a political poem in the ordinary sense would be wrong; not for Blake the crude rhetoric of propaganda, the historian's analysis of the balance of power, economic causes, party loyalties and factions: for him these are but the accidental effects of deep psychological causes. The poem proceeds like a nightmare that unfolds inexorably according to its own inner life. In Swedenborgian terms he writes that '. . . the heavens of France/Perplex'd vibrate round each careful countenance'. The imagery is all of the inner events, a violent world of passions and fear over which reason and calculation have no control. Blake's description of the helplessness and horror of the King of France as these gathering inner collective forces invade him is no less powerful than those images in which the Surrealists attempted to express the inner aspects of our own times:

> . . . Sick, sick, the Prince on his couch, wreath'd in dim
> And appalling mist, his strong hand outstretch'd, from his
>   shoulder down to the bone
> Runs aching cold into the scepter, too heavy for mortal grasp.
>   No more
> To be swayed by visible hand, nor in cruelty bruise the
>   mild flourishing mountains.
> Sick the mountains, and all their vineyards weep, in the
>   eyes of the kingly mourner;
> Pale is the morning cloud in his visage. Rise, Necker!
>   the ancient dawn calls us
> To awake from slumber of five thousand years. I awake,
>   but my soul is in dreams;

From my window I see the old mountains of France, like
aged men, fading away
                    (*The French Revolution*, Lines 2–9, K. 134)

—and so on. It would have been a remarkable political censor who
could have decoded Blake's prophecies into the language of political
sedition; nor indeed does Blake in the ordinary sense 'take sides':
rather in his awe-inspiring vision of war and revolution to come he
bears witness to the downfall of the old order in Europe and the
emergence of a new. He discerned the direction of the flow of
history. In the early Lambeth books we see only the conflicting
forces of Urizen, the aged restrictive law-giver, and Orc, rebellious
spirit of youth, energy and desire. But Blake had not at this time as
yet become aware of the spirit of renewal above and beyond these
conflicting opposites; his early prophecies are a dream of history
rather than a vision of eternity.

We have noted Corbin's important distinction between the
imaginary and the imaginal illumined by spiritual vision. The distinction has always been recognized in the traditional distinction
between dreams that come through the gates of ivory and those
which come through the gates of horn—as we should say from the
personal unconscious and from the transpersonal Self. Surrealism,
much influenced by Freud, is of the former kind; and so to a great
extent are Blake's Lambeth books; they depict with much power the
unconscious forces at work in Europe; they are full of strife and
howlings and groanings, images of constriction and the breaking of
fetters. Perhaps they are not (in Corbin's sense) demonic and destructive as are many surrealist works (in the literal sense of tearing
apart) 'diabolic'; yet they record rather than resolve the turmoil
within the inner worlds. The early Lambeth books contain much
that is now of only historic interest—although there is also much that
is of abiding interest, in part because certain themes are permanent in
the human imagination, but also because some of the problems and
conflicts of the turn of the eighteenth century remain unresolved.
The prevailing secular materialism, represented for Blake by Bacon,
Newton and Locke—the post-Cartesian scientific world-picture
—has only in recent years again been challenged; and it is for this
reason that Blake is at this time so widely proclaimed by a generation
no longer satisfied with the old premises.

But Blake's vision of a higher ordering principle—the Imagination—which 'steps beyond' into a different kind of liberation was to

be the theme of his later and greater books, *Vala or The Four Zoas,
Milton* and *Jerusalem*. In these later books Blake's central concern is
with his own nation, 'the Giant Albion', and above all with London,
his own city, whose inner life he understood so much more nearly
than he could the French Revolution; although indeed his friends
of that time, Thomas Payne and Mary Wollstonecraft were more
nearly and immediately involved; much as in my own youth
students, poets and young intellectuals went to take part in the
Spanish civil war, which had in a similar way captured the imagination of a generation. But Blake was above all the prophet of
London; who speaks to Blake every day and night of his life in his
native city:

'My Streets are my Ideas of Imagination.
'Awake, Albion, Awake! and let us awake up together.
'My Houses are Thoughts: my Inhabitants, Affections,
'The Children of my thoughts walking within my blood-vessels,
'Shut from my nervous form which sleeps upon the verge of
                                                                Beulah
'In dreams of darkness, while my vegetating blood in veiny pipes
'Rolls dreadful through the furnaces of Los and the Mills of Satan.'
                                                                . . .'

So spoke London, immortal Guardian! I heard in Lambeth's
                                                                shades!
In Felpham I heard and saw Visions of Albion.
I write in South Molton Street what I both see and hear
In Regions of Humanity, in London's opening streets.
                                        (*Jerusalem*, Pl. 38, K. 665)

The 'sickness of Albion—his 'deadly sleep'—is, according to
Blake's diagnosis, the materialist philosophy which denies the reality
of the Imagination, 'the true man'. For a race, as for an individual,
denial of the spiritual worlds, the vertical axis of the soul, and the
usurpation of natural reason as supreme ruler and arbiter must
inevitably bring about conflict and rebellion, gnashings and groanings, within the inner worlds. *The Four Zoas*, Blake's first attempt to
discover a resolution of humanity's inner conflicts, is written in
terms of the four battling elements of the soul—reason, feeling, sense
and intuition. Blake had looked into his own inner heavens, there to
discover the 'Four Mighty Ones' who are he says 'in every Man' (a
structure later discerned and elaborated in the psychology of C.G.
Jung). Blake was not, however, only an inspired shaman, he was also

a powerful thinker and in such works as the aphorisms *There is No Natural Religion*, besides his marginalia, letters and other prose statements, we see that he was well able to counter the arguments of Locke and the rest in their own terms. But his insight into the *mundus imaginalis*, the scene of the inner drama and conflict, enabled him to set discursive argument within a larger context, that of the wholeness of Imagination whose unity at once includes and transcends the quaternion. Positivist science was to remain dominant for the whole of the nineteenth century; but his words, neglected in his own lifetime—indeed published for the first time only in the last years of the nineteenth century—were, and are, addressed not to some esoteric élite but to the nation as a whole. With all the eloquence of his poetry, the force of his argument and the skill of his brush, he spoke to the English nation:

> England! awake! awake! awake!
> Jerusalem thy Sister calls!
> Why wilt thou sleep the sleep of death
> And close her from thy ancient walls?

—Jerusalem is the holy city, the city of the soul; and Blake's prophetic mission was to the soul of the nation, fallen into the 'deadly sleep' of materialism. Over the heads of the critics Blake, in his catalogue to his one exhibition of paintings, addresses these 'inhabitants' who walk about in the blood-vessels of London:

> Mr B. appeals to the Public, from the judgment of these narrow blinking eyes which have too long governed art in a dark corner . . .[12]

—and in still stronger words, whose truth that spirit of Time to whose labours Blake bore prophetic witness has nevertheless vindicated,

> There cannot be more than two or three great Painters or Poets in any Age or Country; and these, in a corrupt state of Society, are easily excluded, but not so easily obstructed . . . If Italy is enriched and made great by RAPHAEL, if MICHAEL ANGELO is its supreme glory, if Art is the glory of a Nation, if Genius and Inspiration are the great Origin and Bond of Society, the distinction my Works have obtained from those who best understand

---

[12] Descriptive Catalogue, K. 563.

such things, calls for my Exhibition as the greatest of Duties to my Country.[13]

For Blake the vindication of inspired art is, precisely, its universality. It is universal by virtue of the universal character of Imagination and its innate knowledge. Whereas acquired knowledge is (in Blake's words) a 'fortuitous concourse of memorys accumulated & lost',[14] the 'ever existent images' of the Imagination are common to all. Long before he had written, in *The Marriage of Heaven and Hell*,

Truth can never be told so as to be understood, and not be believ'd[15]

—and so to the end of his life he continued to believe. He criticized the Greek philosophers because they held truth to be discoverable by discursive reason. To the Imagination truth is not by deduction but by recognition. Berkeley in a passage in his *Siris* made, Blake thought, the common mistake of setting reason as arbiter over Imagination; this Blake denied:

Knowledge is not by deduction, but Immediate by Perception or Sense at once. Christ addresses himself to the Man, not to his Reason

—Christ being of course the Imagination; and he added:

Jesus supposes every Thing to be Evident to the Child & to the Poor & Unlearned. Such is the Gospel.[16]

As one who speaks from, and to, the Imagination, the words of the Prophet are not obscure; he addresses that very faculty all share, a universal conscience. Precisely in this lies the prophet's power. As the authority of the scientist lies in the universality of the natural order he discerns, so does the power of the prophet in the universality of a spiritual order; and therein lies the certainty, the irrefutability, of the prophetic word. The vindication of Blake's prophecy is that, unheeded by his contemporaries, he is now universally recognized for what he was. The truth of his diagnosis of the sickness

[13] Advertisement of Exhibition, K. 561.
[14] *Jerusalem*, Pl. 33, K. 659.
[15] Pl. 10, K. 152   [16] K. 774.

of Albion and its inevitable consequences is inclining many to wonder whether the cure also may be that spiritual reawakening for which he laboured; not indeed a religious revival, for Blake had little good to say for 'religion' and its institutions. It is the inspired poet who is 'the awakener', proclaiming, against the domination of natural reason, the wholeness, and therefore the healing power, of the Imagination. Blake makes his type of the inspired poet, 'Milton, the awakener', declare this doctrine:

> To bathe in the Waters of Life, to wash off the Not Human
> I come in Self-annihilation & the grandeur of Inspiration
> To cast aside from Poetry all that is not Inspiration,
> . . .
> To cast off the idiot Questioner who is always questioning
> But never capable of answering, who sits with a sly grin
> Silent plotting when to question, like a thief in a cave
> Who publishes doubt & calls it knowledge, whose science
> is despair.
>
> (Milton, Pl. 41, 1, K. 533)

The prophet speaks not for one single faculty of the mind (reason) but from the wholeness of 'the divine body' of which the Four are agents. When Blake wrote that 'every honest man is a prophet' he by no means meant that 'every man has a right to his own opinion' but, on the contrary, that 'honesty' lies in speaking from the deepest truth of our being—the Imagination. 'I pretend not to holiness,' he wrote, 'yet I pretend to love, to see & to converse with daily as man to man, the more to have an interest with the Friend of Sinners'—again, the Imagination.

V

Throughout the years Blake's understanding of the inner universe clarified and deepened. Whereas in *The French Revolution* we find only the inner aspect of war and conflict and in the Lambeth books the battles of the conflicting Zoas, in those 'deadly dreams' of which history is the perpetual manifestation, we find in *Milton* and *Jerusalem* the continual proclamation of the Imagination. We move from the demonic to the angelic universe, from the 'moving image' to the abiding archetype. In Blake's view the 'fall' of man, his deadly sleep, or amnesis, is the loss of vision of the inner and higher worlds of consciousness, the properly human kingdom.

Refusing to behold the Divine Image which all behold
And live thereby, he is sunk down into a deadly sleep.
                    (*The Four Zoas*, Night the First, ll.290–1, K. 272)

It is the 'divine vision', and above all the archetype of 'the human
form divine'[17] that constitutes man's innate knowledge and lost
guiding principle. Without that guide humankind is bound to the
endless cycle of those 'States of Sleep which the Soul may fall into in
its deadly dreams of Good & Evil when it leaves Paradise following
the Serpent'[18]—the serpent matter and the materialist loss of consciousness. Imagination is not a state, Blake insists, but 'the human
existence itself',

      . . . the Only General and Universal Form
To which all Lineaments tend & seek with love & sympathy.
                    (*Milton*, Pl. 42, K. 672)

Mankind has lost access to the archetype. In an early poem, *Visions of
the Daughters of Albion*, Blake asks why it is that man alone among
living creatures has lost access to his archetype. Chicken and hawk,
bee and mouse, frog and snake, even the blind worm, are guided by
innate wisdom; and the passage ends with the question, central to
Blake's later thought:

And then tell me the thoughts of man, that have been hid of old.
                    (Pl.3, K. 191)

As early as 1788 Blake had written of 'the Poetic Genius' 'which is
every where call'd the Spirit of Prophecy', arguing

   That the Poetic Genius is the true Man, and that the body or
   outward form of Man is derived from the Poetic Genius. Likewise
   that the forms of all things are derived from their Genius, which
   by the Ancients was call'd an Angel & Spirit & Demon.[19]

The prophet, because he speaks from the archetype, must be believed
because that 'general and universal form' is alike in all.

Blake understood the function of the poet in his society to be

[17] *Songs of Innocence*, 'The Divine Image', K. 117.
[18] *Notebook* pp. 91–2, K. 614.
[19] *All Religions are One*, K. 98.

prophetic. Only in so far as art is inspired by the Imagination does it serve any essential function. The widespread loss of the archetype renders the expression of the imaginative vision through the arts an essential need; since poetry, painting, and music are, as Blake says, 'the three Powers in Man of Conversing with Paradise, which the flood did not Sweep away'[20]—the flood being, in Blake's symbolic terms, the deluge of matter—*hyle*, in Neoplatonic terms—the overwhelming of the *mundus imaginalis* by 'the sea of Time and Space'. Religions also, in so far as they are inspired by the imaginative vision, reveal that world:

> The Religions of all Nations are derived from each Nation's different reception of the Poetic Genius, which is every where call'd the Spirit of Prophecy.[21]

Thus the truth of religions, as of inspired poetry, is imaginative truth. From the beginning of his life to the end Blake proclaimed the Imagination as the supreme source of truth. Already in *The Marriage of Heaven and Hell* he had formulated his reason for holding the biblical and prophetic tradition to be superior to the philosophy of the Greeks. He invoked Isaiah and Ezekiel in defence of the prophetic tradition:

> The philosophy of the east taught the first principles of human perception: some nations held one principle for the origin & some another; we of Israel taught that the Poetic Genius (as you now call it) was the first principle and all the others merely derivative, which was the cause of our despising the Priests & Philosophers of other countries and prophecying that all Gods would at last be proved to originate in ours & to be the tributaries of the Poetic Genius.[22]

This, Blake believed, had come to pass; he himself lent his prophetic witness to the supremacy of the innate archetype of the Divine Humanity; and the prophecies of men of genius are self-fulfilling.

This high view of the function of the arts and the office of the poet is inseparable from a certain view of man. In terms of any materialist ideology for which the natural man, called by Blake the 'worm of sixty winters' and 'seventy inches long', whose only knowledge

---

[20] *Notebook*, p. 78, K. 609.
[21] *All Religions are One*, K. 98.   [22] Pl. 12–13, K. 153.

comes through the senses, to be correlated by 'the mind of the ratio', natural reason, is all, cannot, in the terms of a philosophy which makes the mind the passive mirror of a mechanized universe, the Imagination cannot be seen otherwise than (again Blake's words) 'delusion & fancy'.[23] In terms of these ideologies the arts perform no vital function and are at best entertainment or political propaganda. This Blake had clearly seen from the outset, when in 1788 he had written in the margin of his copy of Lavater's *Aphorisms* 'man is either the ark of God or a phantom of the earth & of the water' (K. 82). Have we not but to compare the works of civilizations and societies founded upon the prophetic view that there is a spiritual universe which it is the function of art to celebrate and embody, with the formless or diabolic products of contemporary Western culture, to understand that these are incommensurable? From the living Imagination alone issues that whole treasury of beauty and meaning which can truly be called the expression of the human genius. In his fidelity to this vision of 'the true man' resides the power of the prophet.

[23] *The Four Zoas*, Night the First, l.341, K. 273.

Tennyson and Some Doubts

ALASTAIR THOMSON

At the funeral of Dickens in 1870, Tennyson found it difficult to leave the Abbey after the service, because so many of the immense congregation remained to stare at him, pressing towards the rails of the Sacrarium within which he was sitting. When told what was happening, he insisted on escaping the crowd, and was taken out by a private door. It was a manifestation of his fame that clearly discomposed him. His reputation had been growing steadily for twenty years or more. He was not only the greatest English poet of his age; he was a celebrity, the author not only of *In Memoriam*, but of *Enoch Arden* (which in France was taught, according to Mallarmé, 'dans chaque collège . . . avec notes grammaticales au bas'), and by his own account often troubled in the Isle of Wight retreat which Taine seemed disinclined to forgive him, by rows of staring heads along his garden wall.[1] At the same time there had never been any lack of intelligent adverse criticism. The shrewdest contemporary criticism sometimes comes as a word of caution after the praise, as with Richard Hengist Horne in 1844. Horne's praise is generous, even a little strained, but he notes that 'there is, or appears to be, some vacillation of intention, in his poetry as a mass', and goes on to speak of 'the absence of any marked and perceptible design in his poetical faith and purposes'. 'We seem to look on, while a man stands in preparation for some loftier course . . . He constantly gives us the impression of something greater than his works . . . He may do greater things than he has yet done; but we do not expect it.'[2] Six years later, Tennyson's public found *In Memoriam* a greater thing, but (to adapt Horne slightly) perhaps the public that took *In Memoriam* to its heart would not have done so if its structure had reflected

---

[1] Stéphane Mallarmé, 'Tennyson vu d'ici', *Œuvres Complètes*, eds. Henri Mondor and G. Jean-Aubry (Paris, Gallimard, Bibliothèque de la Pléiade, 1961), pp. 527–31.

[2] Richard Hengist Horne, 'Alfred Tennyson', *The New Spirit of the Age* (London, 1844), II, pp. 3–32; reprinted (abridged) John Jump, ed., *Tennyson: The Critical Heritage* (London, Routledge and Kegan Paul, 1967), pp. 164–5.

more of design in poetical faith and purposes, and had seemed less immediately and appealingly human in its uncertain progress. Much of Tennyson's influence on the age was through *In Memoriam*, and the late idyll *Enoch Arden* of 1864, a long and skilful honouring of the short and simple annals of the poor, with which he enjoyed a huge popular success. He also thought that *Idylls of the King* said something to the age which it needed. In 1887, speaking of modern acts of heroism (he was always fascinated by courage) in spite of the decline of 'the old reverence and chivalrous feeling' in the present age ('this . . . awful moment of transition'), he said, 'the truth is that the wave advances and recedes,' and added 'I tried in my "Idylls" to teach men these things, and the need of the Ideal.'[3] Since the 1940s in particular, many readers have been willing to be taught, and it has been argued that the *Idylls* is one of the great works of the nineteenth century, showing the kingdom of man in its splendid heroism, and inevitable corruption. But moving and intricately fashioned though they are, they are deeply flawed. The critical reassessment of the *Idylls* which has continued over the last thirty years or so has a good deal to do with the recognition that the decline of Tennyson's kingdom is an image of the decline of Western civilization, an anticipation of Spengler and Yeats. It may also have something to do with Britain's marked political decline since the Second World War, and a consequent growing interest (particularly in North America) in a 'matter of Britain', of the sort that we associate with Kipling and David Jones. I suggest this as only one reason why so many critics since the 1940s seem willing to overlook the weaknesses of the *Idylls*.

In Memoriam, on the other hand, offered the experience of a will to faith, transcending the assaults of contemporary science, and made immediate by its form; a hesitant progress towards the concept of a fusion of human, natural, and divine will, and of the presence of the loved dead both in immortal Love, and in star and flower around the living. Whatever the power of the darker sections, there is no mistaking the authority of the resolute turning to take hold, in sections like CVII, or of the feeling for life in the magnificent LXXXVIII ('Wild bird, whose warble, liquid sweet'), with its unwilled participation in the great fullness of life. What removes it farthest from us today is the brooding over all the implications of immortality. And

[3] Hallam Tennyson, *Alfred Lord Tennyson: a Memoir*, 2 vols., 1897: II, p. 337.

Tennyson's thoughts of the crowning human race to come mean little to us now, probably because our first thought of the race to come is that with the risk of nuclear wars it stands a fair chance of not coming at all. There is more immediate interest in the spectacle of the mind's ability to find a way by exploring possibilities, the continual and very human action of supposition, rejection, and more supposition, until some beliefs are clarified, by which we can live.

But although the fear in *In Memoriam* is conquered, and although in the Epilogue he speaks of having 'grown/To something greater than before', we are still left with a sense of a mistrust of self. 'So runs my dream: but what am I?/An infant crying in the night:/An infant crying for the light:/And with no language but a cry': although the poem passes beyond this, the image stays in our mind, not only because of its power, but because of our experience of Tennyson. And together with the absence of design—in the larger sense —which Horne found, there is also a curious uncertainty about the function of poetry itself. It is discernible in a number of poems, but is probably most apparent, not in the sections of *In Memoriam* which seem to slight words or poetry, but in something which on the face of it is a celebration of poetry: *The Epic*, within which he framed the *Morte d'Arthur* for its publication in 1842. This frame is not apologetics designed to forestall criticism of 'faint Homeric echoes'. It is a skilful mediation between poetry and audience which approves the *Morte*, but which also—and in part involuntarily—leaves room for doubt about the place of poetry in the modern age. The setting is 'Francis Allen's on the Christmas-eve', with the host, 'The parson Holmes, the poet Everard Hall', and the narrator, talking late at night after the usual Christmas games are over, and the women have gone to bed. Talk of how the old honour has gone from Christmas leaves the field free for Holmes, who is a bore, and he 'settles down' on 'the general decay of faith/Right through the world', and the lack of any anchor to hold by. Allen presents the diffident Hall as his anchor. Hall, it appears, holds by the wassail-bowl; he burned his Arthurian epic, but the eleventh book that Allen saved from this hearth is brought for him to read, when

> the poet little urged,
> But with some prelude of disparagement,
> Read, mouthing out his hollow oes and aes,
> Deep-chested music, and to this result.

This is not Hall and his wassail-bowl, but 'the poet', and 'Deep-chested music' brings him before us a second before the deep-chested music of the *Morte* itself.

Whereas the introduction is separate from the *Morte d'Arthur*, the conclusion is normally line-numbered consecutively from it. The epic style of 'Here ended Hall', eight lines after the 'So said he' on which the barge that carries Arthur moves out, confirms the man we have not known till now. Holmes has slept, and wakes only to grunt 'Good!'; the age's lateness lives in this decent parsonical bore, 'sent to sleep with sound,/And waked with silence'.

> . . . but we
> Sat rapt: it was the tone with which he read—
> Perhaps some modern touches here and there
> Redeemed it from the charge of nothingness—
> Or else we loved the man, and prized his work;
> I know not: but we sitting, as I said,
> The cock crew loud; as at that time of year
> The lusty bird takes every hour for dawn . . .

Nothing in the reservations after 'rapt' can lessen its force. The crowing of the cock is part of the response, and is so presented: 'but we sat . . . but we sitting, as I said . . .' The reference is to Shakespeare's bird of dawning in *Hamlet*, and though it is not a sign to dispel any doubts in the hearers about whether they did well to be rapt, it is such a sign for us.[4] Nothing more is said, except Allen's muttered 'There now—that's nothing!' as he drives the smouldering log home with more force than usual. But an authentic word has been spoken, by which a change has been wrought. 'And so to bed', where the narrator passes into a dream of Arthur, which towards morning turns to a vision of his return, confirmed by the early Christmas bells.

It is nevertheless difficult to find in *The Epic* unqualified reassurance about poetry in this age, partly because at one moment Tennyson seems to become uncertain of his purpose.[5] Although Hall

---

[4] *Hamlet* I. i. 157–64.

[5] A. Dwight Culler discusses *The Epic* in some detail, in *The Poetry of Tennyson* (New Haven and London, Yale University Press, 1977), pp. 106–9. He takes Allen's holding by Hall to imply an anticipation of Arnold's belief, that in the modern world poetry will come to take the place of religion. It is true that Parson Holmes himself represents the decay of faith, but although Culler's arguments are attractive, there is as much uncertainty as certainty about poetry in *The Epic*.

insists on modernity, that 'a truth/Looks freshest in the fashion of the day', and though his burning of his epic may suggest other things to come, there is an air of defeat about him, and his 'gift' for drinking, that lingers with us despite the deep-chested music, the sitting rapt, and the dream and waking. Of course the self-disparagement and understatement are all very English, and Hall's gift for drinking may mean little one way or the other. Tennyson had something of a gift for port, and frequently exuded an air of defeat, or worse. But we have a feeling that it is not only the old honour of Christmas that has dwindled down to odd nooks like Francis Allen's on the Christmas-eve. What emerges clearly is the homeless state of poetry in this age, and the poet's uncertainty. Allen and the narrator own the effect of poetry: it momentarily changes the world for them, and Tennyson handles this with wonderful skill. But although the dream of Arthur's return is obviously intended to approve this, it fails precisely where it should not, with that part of it which is visionary, and occurs at dawn, when dreams, in a Shakespearean way, 'Begin to feel the truth and stir of day'. 'To me, methought, who waited with a crowd,/There came a bark that, blowing forward, bore/King Arthur, like a modern gentleman/Of stateliest port; and all the people cried,/"Arthur is come again: he cannot die".' 'Methought' is visionary, and the closing lines of *The Epic* remind us of others who have dreamed visions, and waked to Christmas morn and its abiding hope. But the weakness of 'modern gentleman/Of stateliest port' is unmistakable. 'Modern' offers only stiff support to the blank 'gentleman', and 'Of stateliest port' is like a screen hastily trundled forward to cover a mistake. For this reason alone—the failure of the poetry—it is a lying dream, despite the truth and stir of day. It is not merely an aberration on Tennyson's part, offering clumsy proof of something which has already been subtly confirmed. Coming where it does, as a visionary conclusion to a mediation between poetry and audience which demonstrates poetry's enduring power over those who can listen, the orotundity betrays a moment-ary unwillingness in him to trust his own poetry, and with it a hesitancy about poetry itself, of the sort which sometimes looks out at us from *In Memoriam*.

His youthful vision of himself in *Armageddon* had been that of a prophet, a man endowed with extraordinary powers. In the 1829 Cambridge prize poem *Timbuctoo*, made out of *Armageddon* 'by a little alteration of the beginning and the end', the triumph of 'mental excellence', of godlike man capable of vision, is countered by a new

power that reduces everything to the light of common and contemporary day.[6] 'Keen *Discovery*', or exploration, is an analogue of
the enemy of poetry, rational scientific thought concerned with
sight, not vision, which will soon reduce the legendary city from its
glorious ideal state to mud-walled barbarian settlements. But the
full-throated speech of the Spirit of Fable with which the poem ends
is hardly the voice of doubt, or failure. ' "There is no mightier Spirit
than I to sway/The heart of man: and teach him to attain/By
shadowing forth the Unattainable . . ." ' The poem both yields to and
counters doubts about the place and power of poetry, which is
probably one reason why Tennyson called it 'a wild and unmeth-
odized performance'.[7] *The Poet* of 1830 is all orotund declamation,
furnished with the contemporary commonplace of viewless arrows
and wingèd shafts, and many stately but moribund personifications.
Like *The Poet's Mind* of the same year, it is not very far from the level
of the clamorous chauvinism of *English Warsong* (chorus: 'Shout for
England!' etc.) and *National Song* (chorus: 'For the French', etc.). In
some respects *The Hesperides* of 1832 is Tennyson's most uncompromising and most enigmatic statement of the poet's function. The
song of the daughters of Hesperus is the sacred garden expressed in
song, and the complex rhetoric of symbolic opposition (Himala and
Caucasus, Hesper and Phosphor, dragon and demigod, wasted
world and magic apple) grows until it seems to fill the world. It may
or may not be significant that he did not republish it. But in *The
Golden Year*, an English Idyl and a near contemporary of *The Epic*,
the poet Leonard believes he has been born too late, and the weaknesses in his song ('that song which Leonard wrote', not 'made') may
bear him out. Nor is this discredited by the detachment Tennyson
shows, the readiness to take account of other points of view, and
even to make fun of himself. Later, in the 1850s and 1860s, he would
show the destruction of the poet in *Merlin and Vivien*, and *Lucretius*.
Merlin, the great artificer of Camelot, is betrayed by Vivien's hatred
of life, and cunning; Lucretius, by Lucilia's stupidity and cunning:
'And this, at times, she mingled with his drink,/And this destroyed
him . . .' They express a general and growing pessimism in Tennyson, but the strong sexual element in both poems also suggests a deep
sense of vulnerability, which, given their subjects, may indicate a
more particular fear: the failure of the poet in this unpoetic, because

[6] Tennyson, *Memoir* II, p. 355.
[7] Christopher Ricks, ed., *The Poems of Tennyson* (London, Longmans,
1969), p. 172.

divided age; the failure of this poet, in his middle years, to make and shape up to the full height of his powers.

One notable locus for Tennyson's doubts about poetry might seem to be the monologue *Tiresias*, which was partly written in 1833, though not published until 1885, and has obvious affinities with *Ulysses* and *Tithonus*. The occasion is the imminent destruction of Thebes, and Tiresias's urging of Menoeceus, son of Creon, to sacrifice himself and save the city. Its substance is the failure of poetry, and the need for deeds. Prophecy has helped no one, 'Virtue must shape itself in deed'; there is no sound 'so potent to coerce,/And to conciliate' as the names of those who act and die nobly for their country: they are 'a song/Heard in the future'. Nothing could be further from Spenser's classic claim, in *The Ruines of Time* (400–403):

> For deeds doe die, how euer noblie donne,
> And thoughts of men do as themselves decay,
> But wise wordes taught in numbers for to runne,
> Recorded by the Muses, liue for ay.

But it may not seem very far from the sense of Wordsworth's observation, some thirty years before:

> However exalted a notion we would wish to cherish of the character of a Poet, it is obvious, that while he describes and imitates passion, his situation is altogether slavish and mechanical, compared with the freedom and power of real and substantial action and suffering.[8]

Such a comparison would be inappropriate, for *Tiresias* is not Tennyson at his best, being heavily explicatory, and replete with the sense of a large message. 'Thou refusing this,/Unvenerable will thy memory be/While men shall move the lips' is typical of its frequent stiffness. It begins with 'I wish', and the closing movement (whose verse Tennyson admired) opens with 'I would': the heroic action implied is contained within a lament over the lost powers of sight and words. Before his blindness, Tiresias sought everywhere 'the meanings ambushed'; now, having moved Menoeceus to action, he would be where he may find 'the wise man's word,/Here trampled by the populace underfoot,/There crowned with worship.' Here 'Virtue must shape itself in deed, and those/Whom weakness or

---

[8] Wordsworth, Preface to the second edition of *Lyrical Ballads*, 1802.

necessity have cramped/Within themselves, immerging, each, his urn/In his own well, draw solace as he may.' This is central to *Tiresias*, and all too easily heard to be central. Its eloquence is firmly stayed on the legend of Pallas Athene's curse, and its message is delivered as from a rostrum. Given the inferiority of the monologue, we cannot look here for Tennyson's deepest feelings about what poetry could or could not do.

But in *The Lady of Shalott*—if we can for a moment limit its parabolic statement to what it certainly includes—the apparent self-sufficiency of the poetic imagination was shown to be treacherous; the fatality in the poem transcends any suggestion that the artist will do well enough if he sticks to his shadows. There can be no doubt about Tennyson's need to write poetry: it was what he lived for. The rather unequal poems of the 1830s commonly called 'political poems', like *Hail Briton!* and *Of old sat Freedom on the heights*, turn outward. But his deepest need seems to have been for what he could master, and make his own, by which he could make head against the *ennui* and deep depression to which he was subject. It probably brought its own uncertainties with it. Although he is fascinated by spiritual decay, and what moves him most will obviously produce his finest poetry, the exquisite lingering over decay and defeat in the Choric Song of *The Lotos-Eaters*, for example, is implicitly a criticism of poetry itself, which may indicate the real relationship between *The Lotos-Eaters* and *The Hesperides*. 'My words are only words, and moved/Upon the topmost froth of thought': this, from section LII of *In Memoriam*, may not mean more than 'I would that my tongue could utter', or the despair over 'matter-moulded forms of speech' in XCV which other poets besides Tennyson have felt. And although the use V finds in 'measured language' is merely that of 'The sad mechanic exercise,/Like dull narcotics, numbing pain', it is a measure of the pain, that poetry here is no more than that. But again we are left with a feeling that the words have a wider appli-cation, and are not merely a momentary reaction against what he had given his life to. Perhaps the last irony in *Tithonus*, one of the most perfect of his poems, is that of an unspoken comment on language: that this most melodious of lamentations will pass, according to the legend, into the dry chirping of the grasshopper. We must of course distinguish between any apparent hesitation about the value of poetry, and the recognition that the age was late. For that matter, what we may see as signs of a reservation about poetry may be nothing more than a lack of self-confidence in Tennyson. (James

Spedding said of him, 'He seeks for strength not within but without, accusing the baseness of his lot in life and looking to outward circumstances far more than a great man ought to want of them, and certainly more than they will ever bring.'[9]) As for *The Epic*—graceful, modern, allusive—it is haunted by an equal sense of the power of poetry, and its homeless state.

The Poet's Song, the last piece in the 1842 volumes, seems to offer reassurance. In place of the puffing of *The Poet* and the edgy scolding in *The Poet's Mind*, there is a glad evocation of Orphic song.

> The rain had fallen, the Poet arose,
>   He passed by the town and out of the street,
> A light wind blew from the gates of the sun,
>   And waves of shadow went over the wheat,
> And he sat him down in a lonely place,
>   And chanted a melody loud and sweet,
> That made the wild-swan pause in her cloud,
>   And the lark drop down at his feet.
>
> The swallow stopt as he hunted the fly,
>   The snake slipt under a spray,
> The wild hawk stood with the down on his beak,
>   And stared, with his foot on the prey,
> And the nightingale thought, 'I have sung many songs,
>   But never a one so gay,
> For he sings of what the world will be
>   When the years have died away.'

Perhaps there is something of Shelley in it, the Shelley of the *Hymn of Pan*, which also speaks of a magic song and a hushed audience, of birds, insects, and lizards, and which incidentally has a good deal to say about the nature and workings of poetry. It may be the uncharacteristic optimism of its close that makes us think of other poets. The movement, and the mood, are more like Yeats than anyone else: the song the Poet sings is 'gay', and for once a Tennysonian swan is not dying, but only pausing in her cloud. The anapaestic lightness is slowed a little by the absence of rhyme in alternate lines, an absence more marked in the second stanza, which continues the alternation of unrhymed four-beat and rhyming three-beat lines begun at the end of the first stanza. (In 1842 line 9 ended

[9] Quoted by Robert Martin, *Tennyson: The Unquiet Heart* (Oxford, Faber and Faber, 1980), pp. 203–4.

with 'bee'. The correspondence with the 'be' of line 15 was minimal, but he cared enough about it—or the repeated vowel in 'beak' two lines later—to change it to 'fly' in 1888.[10]) The effect of the unrhymed lines is to take the edge off the anapaests, and to leave something open; there is a sense of wonder at what is evoked. But although the conclusion looks forward to a perfected world, the last line still keeps it at something of a tired distance. It seems that Tennyson was in no doubt of what should be sung, even in these later days. His poet's song is a magic song, the essence of world-creating poetry. But the evocation of what is to come is slightly muted, with the lingering thought of the time that has yet to die.

Whatever reservations Arnold had about his powers as a poet, he had few serious doubts about the authority of poetry. Browning, who met the age on something approaching its own terms, gave his testimony in *How It Strikes A Contemporary*, where the age knows nothing of the man who goes quietly up and down, 'Doing the King's work all the dim day long'. Browning knew what it was to be passed over by his contemporaries; Tennyson caught the public imagination at the age of forty-one, and with a few ups and downs held it until his death. The values of his age were probably no more confused than those of ours, which tends to approve itself by feeble satire. On the lowest level—the Queen comes readily to hand as instance—it wanted from poetry eloquent moral and religious guidance confirmed by feeling, and found it almost as easily in Keble's watery *Christian Year* as in *In Memoriam*. Then as now the real assurance was the exquisite subtleties of language and form by which Tennyson is heir to more than twenty centuries of European poetry. But it is some indication of how a later age has wanted to promote him, that he is sometimes called either a Symbolist, or a precursor of the French Symbolists. It is probably not too desperate a simplification to say that Arthur Hallam's 1831 essay on Tennyson (once discredited, now overpraised) has combined with Yeats's interest in it, and with a mistaken idea that Yeats was a Symbolist, to suggest that Tennyson was a Symbolist too. Discussing the 1830 volume, Hallam speaks, with particular reference to *Mariana*, of Tennyson's 'power of embodying himself in ideal characters, or rather moods of character, with such extreme accuracy of adjustment, that the circumstances of the narration seem to have a natural correspondence with the predominant feeling, and, as it were, to be

---

[10] Ricks, ed., p. 736.

evolved from it by assimilative force'.[11] Of this, and some other remarks by Hallam, one critic has remarked that Hallam 'comes astonishingly close to saying in 1831 what we are only now recognizing in the 1970s: Tennyson is essentially a Symbolist poet', and he goes on to say that 'the symbolist technique that Hallam recognized in *Mariana* reaches its farthest development in the *Idylls*'.[12]

Although Symbolism cannot be confined to that of Baudelaire and his successors, it is doubtful whether Tennyson can be called a Symbolist poet, despite the contemporary interest in France in *Idylls of the King*, and despite his influence on Poe, and whatever influence he had through Poe on Baudelaire and Mallarmé. Enough attention has been paid to Tennyson's supposed Symbolism, by Marshall McLuhan and others, to give the question some importance. The Symbolism of that period was essentially a purification of poetry, a release of suggestive powers which had been overlaid and stifled by rhetoric, by which the self could find its true strength in a spiritual world beyond nature. The poem became a separate object or world, both the product and the instrument of visionary purification; it comprehended and passed beyond the phenomenal world, and by it poetry returned to a former condition of incantatory art, or magic. How strict the discipline of Symbolism could be may be seen from the example of Mallarmé, whose art was founded on a concept of the essence of words, who accused Baudelaire, to whose example he had been devoted, of taking reality seriously, and who dreamed of a Work that would be 'the Orphic explanation of the Earth'.[13] It is hardly surprising that Valéry, rightly described by Marcel Raymond as 'the classic of Symbolism', should have remarked, 'Le Symbolisme a peu existé.'[14] But if nothing else it required from its practitioners devotion to poetry as an instrument of power, no matter how that devotion might hide behind the concept of poetry as only a marginal activity of the mind. And although Tennyson lived for

[11] A.H. Hallam, review of *Poems, Chiefly Lyrical, Englishman's Magazine* (31 August 1831), pp. 616–28; reprinted Jump, p. 42.

[12] John D. Rosenberg, *The Fall of Camelot: A Study of Tennyson's Idylls of the King* (Cambridge, Massachusetts, 1973), p. 26.

[13] For Mallarmé's reservations about Baudelaire, see Austin Gill, 'Mallarmé on Baudelaire', in T.V. Benn, ed., *Currents of Thought in French Literature: Essays in Memory of G.T. Clapton* (Oxford, Blackwell, 1965), p. 96.

[14] Paul Valéry, letter to Albert Mockel, May 1918, *Lettres à Quelques-uns* (Paris, Gallimard), p. 128; Marcel Raymond, 'Paul Valéry, or The Classic of Symbolism', *From Baudelaire to Surrealism* (London, Methuen, 1970), pp. 135–51.

poetry, it is hard to discern in him the confidence in it that pre-
supposes the authority of the closed world of the Symbolists. Even
the Romantic concept of a world in which the spirit mingles freely
with things seems alien to him. 'And gazing on thee, sullen tree,/Sick
for thy stubborn hardihood,/I seem to fail from out my blood/And
grow incorporate into thee': behind its force, a sickness of soul and
body almost massive in its conviction—the closing of the Latinate
'incorporate' on the more native 'stubborn hardihood' is arresting, in
more senses than one—is the deep primitive commerce between tree
and man, but it is deathlike, an attempt to escape from the threatened
self. We have only to put Baudelaire's *Les Correspondances* beside
section XLV of *In Memoriam* ('The baby new to earth and sky') to
understand how misleading it is to think of Tennyson as a Symbolist, in spite of *Mariana*. On the one hand, the opening of a world of
signs and profound analogies; on the other, isolation from the
phenomenal world as a sign of maturity:

> So rounds he to a separate mind
>   From whence clear memory may begin,
>   As through the frame that binds him in
> His isolation grows defined.

The nineteenth-century movement from 'the gravitation and the
filial bond/Of Nature' by which Wordsworth's infant Babe 'lives,/
An inmate of this active universe', to the mysterious Symbolist
world 'où de vivants piliers/Laissent parfois sortir de confuses
paroles', is a movement from which Tennyson stands a little aside.
The strain of eighteenth-century Augustanism in his poetry is the
product not of familiarity with things, but of a desire to hold them at
a distance, and it is possible that the recurring theme of the ghostlike
return of those disinherited by long absence owes something to his
often timorous apprehension of the phenomenal world. It rarely
breaks down into chaos: the desolation of *Break, break, break* is that of
an absence of metaphor.[15]

---

[15] It is the failure or refusal to make recognizable fiction which is the
lyric's strength. The essence of the poem is the regularity of the 'Break,
break, break' of the first and last stanzas; the feeling that such regularity must
have meaning; and, in the slow anapaestic lines deriving from and questioning the movement, the inability to find meaning. Even the attempted
apprehension of 'thy cold gray stones' in the first stanza turns at the end to
the dry 'at the foot of thy crags'. What the lyric perfectly expresses is the fact
of loss in a world which gives neither metaphors nor reasons.

The corollary of the strong mistrust of self in Tennyson (which may account in part for his passionate desire to believe in immortality) is an unwillingness to confront what is there on his own terms. ('What the devil do you suppose the Duke wants to see me for?' he said roughly to Monckton Milnes, who had offered to introduce him to his hero, the Duke of Wellington.[16]) And it is difficult to reconcile with the assurance of Symbolism, its grasp of the phenomenal before it moves beyond it, the fear, in *Parnassus*, of the new and terrible Muses, Astronomy and Geology, or his later habit of expecting from his friends ideas or subjects for poetry. In spite of resemblances like that between Mallarmé's 'Je me mire et me vois Ange!' (*Les Fenêtres*), and Tennyson's youthful 'I felt my soul grow godlike . . . seemed to stand/Upon the outward verge and bound alone/Of God's omniscience' (*Armageddon*), there are only occasional moments in common between him and the nineteenth-century Symbolists. Sometimes a jewelled passage will suggest the coruscating style affected by some Symbolists.

>   Can thy love,
> Thy beauty, make amends, though even now,
> Close over us, the silver star, thy guide,
> Shines in those tremulous eyes that fill with tears
> To hear me?

Tithonus's question trembles between knowledge of his fate, and a refusal to accept it, and the final and ominous answer lies not in Aurora's tears, but in the star which they reflect. The tiny silver star is the 'alma Venus' or nurturing Venus of Lucretius, 'quae terras frugiferentis concelebras': 'who fillest with thyself the earth with her kindly fruits'; the goddess of Nature, so presented in *Lucretius*, as in the great poem from which *Lucretius* derives, who will not, even if she could, forgive the mortal who has escaped the cycle of death and rebirth. Her power is contained by the periphrasis of 'the silver star', and by the tiny brilliant reflection itself, at once near, and very far, and ominously near in meaning. Its containment, and its radiation— by the containment itself, as by the nature of the image and its exactly central position in these lines—has a jewel-like intensity. This is an effect that Tennyson is master of, but its intensity is Alexandrian, not Symbolist.

Parnassus, written in 1889, three years before his death, is essen-

---

[16] Quoted by Martin, p. 243.

tially a cry of despair before the advance of science. Despite the epigraph from Horace's 'Exegi monumentum aere perennius', the reassurance of the close (an afterthought) is rather weak. The poet will always sing ('Other songs for other worlds!'), but somehow the question of what he will sing thrusts up from behind that 'other'. The assurance of *Merlin and the Gleam* in the same year is that of a quest in which he has not faltered. But in *The Voice and the Peak* of 1874 he had shown a different kind of assurance. This is the period of *Balin and Balan*, one of the most subtly parabolic of all Tennyson's poems, and the terms of this short meditative poem could deceive us into thinking that here at least Tennyson is on the highroad to *le Symbolisme*. (It is also the period of the Metaphysical Society, to which he contributed *The Higher Pantheism* in 1869, and whose collapse in 1879 he said was due to the fact that 'after ten years of strenuous effort no one had succeeded in even defining the term "Metaphysics" '.[17])

I

The voice and the Peak
   Far over summit and lawn,
The lone glow and long roar
   Green-rushing from the rosy thrones of dawn!

II

All night have I heard the voice
   Rave over the rocky bar,
But thou wert silent in heaven,
   Above thee glided the star.

III

Hast thou no voice, O Peak,
   That standest high above all?
'I am the voice of the Peak,
   I roar and rave for I fall.

IV

'A thousand voices go
   To North, South, East, and West;
They leave the heights and are troubled,
   And moan and sink to their rest.

[17] *Memoir* II, p. 170.

V

'The fields are fair beside them,
   The chestnut towers in his bloom;
But they—they feel the desire of the deep—
   Fall, and follow their doom.

VI

'The deep has power on the height,
   And the height has power on the deep;
They are raised for ever and ever,
   And sink again into sleep.'

VII

Not raised for ever and ever,
   But when their cycle is o'er,
The valley, the voice, the peak, the star
   Pass, and are found no more.

VIII

The Peak is high and flushed
   At his highest with sunrise fire;
The Peak is high, and the stars are high,
   And the thought of a man is higher.

IX

A deep below the deep,
   And a height beyond the height!
Our hearing is not hearing,
   And our seeing is not sight.

X

The voice and the Peak
   Far into heaven withdrawn,
The lone glow and long roar
   Green-rushing from the rosy thrones of dawn!

The structure is more complex than might at first appear. The pure image of I, undisturbed by any verb, ends in what seems to be the outmoded diction of 'the rosy thrones of dawn', and 'Hast thou no voice, O Peak?' is the characteristic tone of an earlier generation of poets, of Coleridge or Shelley before Mont Blanc, which had a voice for each of them. But the voice Tennyson hears has nothing to do with rejoicing, or with mild and serene faith: it is that of the natural effect of height and depth, in the stream he has heard all night, which will now deny him whatever vision he seeks in favour of its own sum of knowledge. What follows is the decorative instance, so extended as almost to justify Ruskin's creation of the pathetic fallacy, of troubled voices with the desire of the deep on them, and the final cycle of interchange between deep and height. A third-rate poet would have stopped there, and in fact stanzas I–VI are like a version by Tennyson of an inferior poem made up of observation, and moral. VII begins a farther stage, denying the easy solution of the for ever and ever of the stream's cycle. (On the evidence of VI and VII, this meditation at daybreak renews some of the thinking in the 1830 pendant poems, *Nothing Will Die* and *All Things Will Die*.) VIII confirms the advance, but its ballad-like style croons over the height of man's thought in a way reminiscent of W.E. Henley and other users of ballad effects to support large claims. (The MS first reading of line 16 shows that IV originally had something of the same effect: 'They leave the height and are troubled,/They roar till they find a rest.'[18]) And IX, in the language of *The Higher Pantheism*—'the ear of man cannot hear, and the eye of man cannot see'—sets its seal on this. But meanwhile,

> The voice and the Peak,
> Far into heaven withdrawn . . .

The experience of the first six stanzas, even that of 'the thought of a man', has mysteriously retired (voice as well as Peak) into a much farther heaven than that of II, and the hearing and seeing that the poem began with are now vision. We are left with the first and last of knowledge, in the inviolate symbol.[19]

---

[18] Ricks ed., p. 1222.
[19] The form of the first and last stanzas, which present this knowledge, differs slightly. I read 3 as 'The lóne glów and lóng roár', which means that the lines of the stanza lengthen regularly from 1 to 4, which is a normal heroic line; unlike the other iambics in the anapaestic rhythm of the poem, it remains uncompromisingly iambic. If these variations, and the stanza's metrical expansion mean anything at all, they may suggest by the end of the poem either the authority, and the resources, of poetry, or the close, and sometimes unavailing grapple with the symbol with which it began. In the matter of symbol and Symbolism, it may be worth noting that the equal stress in 3 on adjective and noun, together with the similarity of sound in 'lone' and 'long', has the effect of blurring distinctions.

The structure of the poem may therefore also be seen as a process by which the difficulty and the rare authority of poetry make themselves known. It suggests that poetry is not extended conceits, however rational their basis, perhaps that it is not mere abyss-mongering either, and that its essence is in symbol. So much at least Tennyson has in common with the Symbolists, but it is no paradox to say that it is little enough. The poem also demonstrates that there is a language which is not the language of every day, and which must be honoured: the 'rosy thrones of dawn' which begins as stagey periphrasis ends by having meaning, because of the poem's energy. The suggestion and the demonstration are the more welcome, from the hand of the sixty-four-year-old Victorian master who sometimes doubted the value of his craft.

Yeats: The Poet as Hero

SUHEIL BUSHRUI

And I would have all know that when all falls
In ruin, poetry calls out in joy,
Being the scattering hand, the bursting pod,
The victim's joy among the holy flame,
God's laughter at the shattering of the world.
(W.B. Yeats, 'The King's Threshold', *Collected Plays*, p. 114)

I

In the early 1900s, when Yeats was moving away from the Pre-Raphaelism of his early verse and developing into a modern poet, his only rivals as serious poets were the innocuous Georgians. It was at this time that Yeats was developing his conviction that the poet had an important responsibility to his society. I shall show in this paper how this conviction informed as it were Yeats's 'Defence of Poetry', and inspired his advocacy of the heroic character of the poet, as seen in his play, *The King's Threshold*.

The King's Threshold was first published in 1904; although it underwent at least two major revisions, in 1906 and 1922, the original proclamation of the absolute value of poetry remained unchanged as the central concern of the play.

Apart from the success of *The King's Threshold* as a drama, it is the first work in which Yeats's theories on poetry and the place of the poet in national life are imaginatively presented. In addition, *The King's Threshold* can be considered as Yeats's own 'Defence of Poetry' as well as being an important statement of his heroic ideal. I hope to show in this paper how the two aspects are mutually inclusive for Yeats, how the defence of poetry and the poet as a hero are axiomatic for him.

The play centres upon Seanchan, the poet at the Court of King Guaire, and his hunger-strike in protest against the King's bid to restrict the ancient rights of the poet. Various characters, each with a different sort of temptation, attempt to make the poet eat but fail in their efforts. Finally the poet dies mourned by his pupils and sweetheart. The conflict between the power of poetry, represented by the prostrate figure of the poet Seanchan, is further emphasized by the setting, which remains constant throughout the play.

In striking contrast to most of Yeats's earlier dramas, *The King's Threshold* was almost topical in its appeal. Yeats wrote it to vindicate the claims of the poet, which had been challenged by politicians and moralists. His revisions of the play were in turn influenced by events between 1903 and 1905, and 1920 and 1922, in the Irish literary and theatrical world, and Irish politics respectively. The press attacks against his theatre and J.M. Synge account partly for his almost savage defence of the rights and the functions of the poet.

Having already been attacked by 'the Pulpit and the Newspapers' over *The Countess Cathleen*, as early as 1899, Yeats made it clear in *Samhain* in 1901 that his theatre was going to 'make no promises'[1] to any section of the community. A year later he repeated what was to be his established conviction: 'the creation of an emotion of beauty is the only kind of literature that justifies itself.'[2]

New attacks only strengthened him in a personal crusade on behalf of the cause of beauty and literature. A note to *The King's Threshold* of 1906 recalls Yeats's bitter struggle:

> It was written when our Society was having a hard fight for the recognition of pure art in a community of which one half was buried in the practical affairs of life, and the other half in politics and a propagandist patriotism.[3]

Yeats rewrote, in particular, the parts of the Monk, the Soldier, and the Mayor, giving them a greater narrow-mindedness and hatefulness that reflected the scars of battle.

The final revisions of 1922 are concerned almost solely with the last scene, and strengthen even further the heroic posture of Seanchan. For here Yeats changed the earlier ending to conform with his original tragic conceptions which he had altered, as he later testified, on a friend's advice. In the latest version Seanchan dies: the enemies of poetry are apparently triumphant, and only the poet's pupils and sweetheart are left to pay him a last tribute. But the King's triumph is worldly, like the poet's defeat: what really matters is the ultimate

---

[1] W.B. Yeats, *Explorations*, selected by Mrs. W.B. Yeats (London, Macmillan, 1962), p. 83.

[2] Ibid., p. 93.

[3] W.B. Yeats, *Poems, 1899–1905* (London, Bullen, 1906), p. 279.

victory which transcends the enmity of time and the forces of destruction. The pupils inherit Seanchan's legacy; his death, far from putting an end to the struggle, has raised it to a heroic level. Seanchan's sacrifice is the beginning of a new life, a new race of man, a new civilization:

> The heroic act, as it descends through tradition, is an act done because a man is himself, because, being himself, he can ask nothing of other men but room amid remembered tragedies; a sacrifice of himself, almost, so little may he bargain, of the moment to the moment.[4]

II

To what extent then is the heroic ideal important for Yeats; along what lines does Yeats develop his theory of Poetry; and in what way do these two elements become the central vision of the play?

The importance of the heroic ideal in Yeats's poetic theory and general thought is well treated in Alex Zwerdling's book.[5] The main thesis of Zwerdling's work is that, in reaction to the development of the democratic and materialist trends of twentieth-century society, with, as Yeats saw it, its destruction of the imaginative, heroic ideals that had previously inspired the greatest art, Yeats reverted:

> to the more primitive stages of hero-worship, to the mythological hero in his visionary poems; to the epic and tragic hero in his use of the Irish heroic cycles.[6]

In a word, Zwerdling sees Yeats's heroic ideal as 'violently, as deliberately nostalgic and anachronistic'.[7] The accent is therefore on the type of hero which Zwerdling associates with primitive society; the individualist hero, whose end is self-fulfilment rather than the social good. Such a hero, in contrast to the nineteenth-century social heroes who inspired exemplification, or to the modern anti-hero whose worldliness is heavily stressed, is above ordinary humanity: as Cuchulain, he excites wonder and admiration.

Zwerdling's emphasis is quite accurate, and the variation of this theme which he observes in Yeats's public heroes, such as Parnell, and his aristocratic heroes, like Robert Gregory, is generally apt.

---

[4] Yeats, *Explorations,* p. 375.
[5] Alex Zwerdling, *Yeats and the Heroic Ideal.*
[6] Ibid., p. 8.
[7] Ibid.

However, what he does not make explicit, and what I hope to establish here, is that the Yeatsian hero displays above all moral courage and vision. We shall see how Seanchan displays both these qualities in his defence of poetry in *The King's Threshold*.

Another source to which reference should be made is Thomas Carlyle. As Zwerdling notes, Yeats condemned Carlyle for his 'ill-breeding and theatricality',[8] but the differences between these two great though dissimilar writers are those of personality rather than principle in the matter of hero-worship. In the case of Cromwell, Yeats evidently loathed Carlyle's choice of hero, for he saw him as the harbinger of the modern egalitarianism he associates with the murder of the aristocratic ideal, as in 'The Curse of Cromwell':

> You ask what I have found, and far and wide I go:
> Nothing but Cromwell's house and Cromwell's murderous crew,
> The lovers and the dancers are beaten into the clay,
> And the tall men and the swordsmen and the horsemen,
> Where are they?[9]

It is true that for much of his life Carlyle's hero was a social hero who gave up self in order to serve society. But individuality in the Carlylean hero is far more marked than in any other Victorian examples. Also, the similarity in the development of Carlyle's and Yeats's social philosophy, under equivalent stresses, is remarkable. As he grew older, Carlyle's contempt for Victorian materialism and 'stump-orator democracy' led him to as fierce and as aristocratic as well as 'anachronistic' a concept of heroism as Yeats. Exchange Old Norse myth for Old Irish myth, and the Norman warrior-aristocracy of William the Conqueror for its Anglo-Irish descendants, and the common ground is clear.

An evident factor to remark, however, is Carlyle's ranking of the hero above the poet. For him the hero is the great man *per se*: the implication is that he might *be* anything, for the essential factor in his greatness is that he has seen deeply into Nature and discovered her laws. This will often invest him with a quality of language which other men do not possess: 'Napoleon has words in him which are like Austerlitz battles.'[10] Yet he may, on the other hand, be unable

---

[8] W.B. Yeats, *Essays and Introductions* (London, Macmillan, 1961), p. 236.

[9] W.B. Yeats, *Collected Poems* (London, Macmillan, 1961), p. 350.

[10] Thomas Carlyle, *On Heroes and Hero-Worship* (London, Chapman & Hall, 1897), p. 79.

to express his understanding in articulate words, like Carlyle's Muhammad and Cromwell. But this is not to be held against him, for if his language be not poetical, his actions will be, which is all the better. Heroic activity is of the essence with Carlyle, for when the hero incarnates the heroic essence in the form of the poet, the potentially active is understood: 'He could not sing the Heroic Warrior, unless he himself were at least a Heroic Warrior too.'[11] The difference, then, is that for Carlyle it is the hero who comes first, whereas for Yeats it is the poet. Yeats would have admitted no distinction: the poet *is* hero. For Carlyle also, the hero invariably has the stuff of poetry in him. Carlyle worships the inarticulate most; Yeats loved eloquence and rhetoric.

When we turn to Yeats's actual 'defence of poetry' as seen in *The King's Threshold*, we can see that his theory fuses Neo-Classical and Romantic poetic creeds. He draws initially on traditional models, Blake and Shelley influencing him directly; for he agreed with Blake that literature and the imaginative arts were 'the greatest of Divine Revelations';[12] and with Shelley that 'the poet and the law-giver hold their station by the right of the same faculty, the one uttering in words and the other in the forms of society, his vision of the divine order, the Intellectual Beauty'.[13] Here Yeats follows his English predecessors of the nineteenth century; but as he takes up this tradition it is transformed by his reading in French Symbolist theories, his addiction to aestheticism, and his loyalty to Irish Nationalism. His membership of the Rhymers' Club in the 1890s and his acquaintance with the leading figures of the aesthetic movement, in addition to the influence of other contemporaries, developed in him a rigorous concern with craftsmanship and made him aim at formal perfection. However, this was not for the sake of art only, but for 'the image of human perfection' which he felt was the aim of art. 'All art is in the last analysis an endeavour to condense as out of the flying vapour of the world an image of human perfection, and for its own and not for the art's sake.'[14] This theory of poetry, which Yeats based on the great English tradition, had become completely personal by 1904, when he added his own contribution. This emphasizes the place of poetry in the life of the nation, past, present and future, relates it to an aristocratic conception of the artist, and links the whole with certain Nietzschean ideas.

[11] Ibid.   [12] Yeats, *Essays and Introductions*, p. 112.   [13] Ibid.
[14] Yeats, *Poems, 1899–1905*, pp. xii–xiii.

III

The King's Threshold is therefore 'no half apologetic "defence of poetry", no sweet and reasonable plea for its acceptance or deferential statement of its function'.[15] Like Shelley's *Defence of Poetry*, it is:

> a flaming exultation of that vision which is the symbol of all spiritual knowledge and the gift of the spirit beside which all other values are disvalued. Poetry is either the root of life, or it is nothing. And so no compromise, however seemingly honourable, can be considered, whether from kings or counsellor, lover or disciples.[16]

The poet is vindicated against the representatives of the 'reasoners and merchants' and of the 'unmitigated exercise of the calculating faculty'.

Milton and Shelley based their claims for the poet on an older tradition and were inspired by Greek, and particularly Platonic, theories. Similarly Yeats based his claims for the poet not only on the tradition upheld by Milton and Shelley, but on the tradition of Ancient Ireland, where the Court Poet was a wielder of real power. It pleased him to find that 'ancient Ireland knew it all', and that a poet was the guardian of traditional order, the protector of the realm, the oracle of ancient wisdom, as well as one who rendered men and their deeds immortal.

In *The King's Threshold* poetry is said to be:

> One of the fragile, mighty things of God,
> That die at an insult.[17]

Poetry is the root of life, and what we call heroism, immortality, joy, valour, love, and magnanimity are meaningless without the meaning poetry attached to them. Poetry is heroic, because it transforms what may seem defeat into triumph:

> Cry out that not a man alive
> Would ride among the arrows with high heart,
> Or scatter with an open hand, had not
> Our heady craft commended wasteful virtues.   (p. 127)

[15] Una Ellis-Fermor, *The Irish Dramatic Movement* (London, Methuen, 1913), p. 93.   [16] Ibid.

[17] W.B. Yeats, *Collected Plays* (London, Macmillan, 1960); hereafter quotations from *The King's Threshold* appear in text.

If we were to deny poetry its right, or give it second place in the order of things, this would mean the death, not only of what are commonly called the arts, but of the great generative art of life itself:

> If I had eaten when you bid me, sweetheart,
> The kiss of multitudes in times to come
> Had been the poorer.
>
> (p. 139)

Kingship too is dependent on the poet for its prestige and preservation:

> And how could they be born to majesty
> If I had never made the golden cradle?
>
> (p. 113)

Thus the supremacy of poetry is asserted: it sets the image and high ideals to which successive generations mould themselves. Man has been created in God's image, and every nation and generation is also created in an image divinely inspired. This image or ideal is a revelation manifested in poetry and the poet's vision. When the Oldest Pupil is asked by his master what made poetry necessary, he repeats an old lesson, saying:

> I said the poets hung
> Images of the life that was in Eden
> About the child-bed of the world, that it,
> Looking upon those images, might bear
> Triumphant children.
>
> (pp. 111–12)

The poet has a real part to play in generation, as well as regeneration.

Without that ideal or image in whose shape a nation must be born, there will be nothing but deformity and ugliness:

> If the Arts should perish,
> The world that lacked them would be like a woman
> That, looking on the cloven lip of a hare,
> Brings forth a hare-lipped child.
>
> (p. 112)

For Yeats physical beauty was not accidental, but the product of long soul-toil, and ugliness of intellect was as much a deformity as that of the body. 'Adam's Curse', for example, parallels the labour of the artist in creating beauty and the labour of the woman to be beautiful:

> Better go down upon your marrow-bones
> And scrub a kitchen pavement, or break stones
> Like an old pauper, in all kinds of weather;
> For to articulate sweet sounds together
> Is to work harder than all these . . .
> . . . To be born woman is to know—
> Although they do not talk of it at school—
> That we must labour to be beautiful.[18]

The labour of both artist and woman was heroic: Yeats believed in a very close connection between the intellect and the body:

> All dreams of the soul
> End in a beautiful man's or woman's body.[19]

These ideas are dramatized when Seanchan reminds the Court Ladies that beauty has been conferred on them by the images the poet gave their mothers:

> You're fair to look upon.
> Your feet delight in dancing, and your mouths
> In the slow smiling that awakens love.
> The mothers that have borne you mated rightly.
> They'd little ears as thirsty as your ears
> For many love songs.
>
> (p. 130)

And again these girls are 'beautiful' because the poet has created their image in the minds of the young men:

> But it is I that am singing you away
> Singing you to the young men.
>
> (p. 130)

On the other hand, the Cripples stand in contrast to the beautiful Court Ladies. They symbolize the corruption and deformity threatening a community that has denied the power of the imagination and

---

[18] Yeats, *Collected Poems*, p. 89.   [19] Ibid., p. 186.

their symbolic value is emphasized by the poet's own wonder at their deformity:

> But why were you born crooked?
> What bad poet did your mothers listen to
> That you were born so crooked?
>
> (p. 133)

So poetry creates man's environment, his life and ideals. It is the language through which God speaks to man, and the poet is but a mirror in which God's splendour is reflected. The act of poetic creation is hardly less remarkable than that of divine creation. Yet it requires heroic labour as we have seen:

> A line will take us hours maybe;
> Yet if it does not seem a moment's thought,
> Our stitching and unstitching has been naught.[20]

Further, it requires vision and deliberation; in 'The Long-Legged Fly' Yeats conceived of the following image of silent, heroic creativity:

> There on that scaffolding reclines
> Michael Angelo.
> With no more sound than the mice make
> His hand moves to and fro.
> Like a long-legged fly upon the stream
> His mind moves upon silence.[21]

No less important, as *The King's Threshold* bears out, than the ability to create fine poetry, the poet and artist must have the highest estimation of his art and the moral courage to stand by it.

The King's Threshold leaves no doubt that Yeats considers the poet's function supreme. Poetry and art can never be servants; they can only be masters, and they are above nationalism, perhaps above the people themselves. Yeats wished to assert, not only 'that the poet is as important to society as is the man of action, but also to assert that poetry cultivated for its own sake, the sake of art, is as necessary to a nation, to Ireland, as what Ireland calls patriotism'.[22]

---

[20] Ibid., p. 88.   [21] Ibid., p. 382.
[22] Cornelius Weygandt, *Irish Plays and Playwrights* (London, Constable, 1913), pp. 60–1.

The poet is indeed most patriotic when he serves only his art; this service must take precedence over all else. The definition Yeats gave of a true Nationalist in 1903 explains his refusal to turn his art or his theatre into a political instrument, as Arthur Griffith and Maud Gonne had wished. The Nationalists had challenged his right to call his theatre 'National', and he replied:

> A good Nationalist is, I suppose, one who is ready to give up a great deal that he may preserve to his country whatever part of her possessions he is best fitted to guard.[23]

The possessions which the poet is best fitted to guard are those values and ideals without which a nation cannot survive. These were precious to Yeats, and he was amazed and indignant that institutions and newspapers, which to him were but the 'voice of the mob',[24] should sit in judgement on literature and art; thus he wrote in *Samhain* of 1903; 'My objection was to the rough-and-ready conscience of the newspapers and the pulpit in a matter so delicate and so difficult as literature.' Poetry, unlike the pulpit and the newspapers, is not intended for propaganda: the only propaganda the poet or the artist could accept was that 'of good art':[25]

> We have no gift to set a statesman right;
> He has had enough of meddling who can please
> A young girl in the indolence of her youth,
> Or an old man upon a winter's night.[26]

When the question of ecclesiastical censorship arose in the early years of the Irish Literary Theatre, in 1901, Yeats's position was made clear in a letter to the *Freeman's Journal,* in which he had rejected the censorship proposed by Moore:

> I believe that literature is the principal voice of the conscience, and it is its duty age after age to affirm its morality against the special moralities of clergymen and churches, and of kings and parliaments and peoples. But I do not expect this opinion to be the opinion of the majority of any country for generations, and it may always be the opinion of a very small minority.[27]

---

[23] Yeats, *Explorations*, p. 118.   [24] Ibid., p. 112.
[25] Ibid., p. 111.   [26] Yeats, *Collected Poems*, p. 175.
[27] *The Letters of W.B. Yeats*, edited by Alan Wade (London, R. Hart-Davis, 1954), p. 356, 14 November, 1901.

That this problem occupied Yeats throughout his life is clear from
one of his later poems 'Church and State' written in 1934:

> Here is fresh matter, poet,
> Matter for old age meet;
> Might of the Church and the State,
> Their mobs put under their feet.
> O but heart's wine shall run pure,
> Mind's bread grow sweet.
>
> That were a cowardly song,
> Wander in dreams no more;
> What if the Church and the State
> Are the mob that howls at the door!
> Wine shall run thick to the end,
> Bread taste sour.[28]

The 'wine' and 'bread' imagery so wonderfully used here can be
traced to *The King's Threshold*, where Seanchan refused 'bread' and
'wine' offered him by Fedelm, the poet's sweetheart, and his other
tempters.

In *The King's Threshold* Yeats's position is quite uncompromising;
his experience had taught him that neither Church nor State could be
trusted and that Poetry alone could give Ireland what was most
needed: intellectual and spiritual rebirth. He bore the burden of this
realization through the crises of the National Theatre Society, the
Lane Pictures affair, and the birth of the new Irish State. Particularly
in *Responsibilities* he began to develop his personal heroic rhetoric
and mythology against the materialist and narrowly sectarian ethos,
as he saw it, of the new Ireland. He repeated here Seanchan's claim
that 'only the wasteful virtues earn the sun', and in so doing made
the expression of his position even more defiant and outspoken.
Although it is true that Yeats's heroic ideal became all the more
individualist and self-fulfilling, behind it we can see the same vision
that Seanchan first presented in *The King's Threshold*: the poet and
the values he creates must be supreme. The artist stands above the
vulgar judgement of the populace:

> And Guidobaldo, when he made
> That grammar school of courtesies
> Where wit and beauty learned their trade

---

[28] Yeats, *Collected Poems*, p. 327.

Upon Urbino's windy hill,
Had sent no runners to and fro
That he might learn the shepherds' will.[29]

Yeats's Irish Nationalism gave a new meaning to the accepted importance of poets in the life of a nation. The Irish and Anglo-Irish traditions also led him to introduce new elements concerning the poet's place in society. *The King's Threshold* contains an image of the relationship that should exist between the poet and the Court, which represents the Government or State. Here Yeats was influenced by what he had read in Geoffrey Keating's bardic history of Ireland written about 1640. This relationship was also hinted at in Lady Wilde's version of the legend on which *The King's Threshold* seems to be based.[30] The revisions of 1922 emphasize this aspect of the play; the change of 'table' into 'council' or 'great council' signifies the governing body, the source of authority.

This authority is as sacred as poetry and should therefore be purified from all mediocre influences. That is why Seanchan does not seek to do away with the Court or Kingship; on the contrary, he is anxious to strengthen their roots and allow them to fulfil their divinely ordained role. He is intent on ridding the Court of those destructive forces that may overcome it and usurp its authority. These forces are represented by the 'Bishops, Soldiers and Makers of the Law', who in Yeats's mind stood for 'middle-class' culture, with its intellectual inadequacies.[31] The Court (or State) should be the poet's patron and allow him to fulfil himself without forcing him in any way; and it should, at all times, shelter him from the vulgarity of popular demands. Seanchan has always taught his pupils to revere the Court:

Upon that day he spoke about the Court,
And called it the first comely child of the world,
And said that all that was insulted there
The world insulted, for the Courtly life
Is the world's model.

(p. 113)

[29] Ibid., p. 120.
[30] Lady Wilde, *Ancient Legends, Mystic Charms and Superstitions of Ireland* (London, Chatto and Windus), p. 159.
[31] 'It is the change, that followed the Renaissance and was completed by newspapers, government and scientific movement, that has brought upon us all these phrases and generalizations made by minds that would grasp what they have never seen' (Yeats, *Explorations*, p. 149).

And the Chamberlain speaks of the Court in the following terms:

> Have you no respect
> For this worn stair, this all but sacred door,
> Where suppliants and tributary kings
> Have passed, and the world's glory knelt in silence?
> Have you no reverence for what all other men
> Hold honourable?
>
> (p. 121)

The Court is an image of beauty and order which begets its own image through being contemplated; but it is once again an image originally created by the poet himself. Poetry is the life-force behind the Court: take poetry away and the whole image will be distorted by ugliness and disease. The Poet and the Court collaborate to make a better world, and in a sense complete each other.

Closely related to this idea of the Court and the poet's place in it is Yeats's belief in aristocracy. Later he identified it with Anglo-Irish tradition, in which Swift, Berkeley, Goldsmith, and Burke formed an aristocracy of intelligence. The Court is sustained and upheld by an enlightened aristocracy—the 'big house' tradition—which extends to the poet its courtesy and patronage. Coole Park and the Court of Urbino celebrated by Castiglione were aspects of the same ideal. Coole Park was a living image of his aristocratic world, and thus also an image from another age, come to life at a time when he had desperately repeated the cry that 'all things at one common level lie'. It would be worth considering how Yeats would have developed, had he not found in Lady Gregory and Coole Park the patron and surroundings a poet of Shakespeare's time might have enjoyed.

Yeats believed that the tradition of courtly patronage would allow the poet to create in an atmosphere of 'leisure and contemplation'. Some years later he wrote that:

> Neither poetry nor any subjective art can exist but for those who do in some measure share its traditional knowledge, a knowledge learned in leisure and contemplation.[32]

The relationship between the poet and his patron (whether it be the Court, the State, or a great house) is one in which there must be complete freedom for the poet. He should never be forced to stoop

---

[32] Yeats, *Explorations*, p. 251.

intellectually or artistically and 'never make a poorer song that he might have a heavier purse'.[33] The artist should possess that 'capricious spirit' which is free like the wind and 'bloweth as it listeth'. This is the point which Seanchan tries to make the Chamberlain understand: the contrast between a free poet (Seanchan) and a servile one (Chamberlain); and the fact that servility can never create beauty:

Chamberlain   You mean we have driven poetry away
                  But that's not altogether true, for I,
                  As you should know, have written poetry.
                  And often when the table has been cleared,
                  And candles lighted, the King calls for me,
                  And I repeat it him. My poetry.
                  Is not to be compared with yours; but still,
                  Where I am honoured, poetry, in some measure,
                  Is honoured too.

Seanchan   Well, if you are a poet,
                  Cry out that the King's money would not buy,
                  Nor the high circle consecrate his head,
                  If poets had never christened gold, and even
                  The moon's poor daughter, that most whey-faced
                                                          metal,
                  Precious . . .

                                                          (p. 127)

Yeats's aristocratic system is founded upon certain values which are intended to influence the life of a nation. Dignity, nobility, and reverence—'Traditional sanctity and loveliness'—based on custom and ceremony, pomp and ritual, are the most striking characteristics of this system.[34] These ideas were developed over the years by Yeats, but they can all be found in germ in *The King's Threshold*.

Tradition, for example, gives the poet his authority, and strengthens that of the Court; that is why the poet objects to the abrogation of an 'ancient right' which was 'Established at the establishment of the world'. Poetry is as eternal as the sun and the moon, it is unchangeable, though it brings about change; for it 'Can hurry beyond Time and Fate and Change'.[35]

[33] Yeats, *Collected Poems*, p. 116.
[34] Ibid., p. 214.
[35] This line present in all earlier versions of *The King's Threshold* is omitted in 1934.

IV

Both Yeats's aristocratic conception of the artist and his theory of poetry and tragedy were strongly influenced by certain Nietzschean ideas. Just as his unravelling of Blake's symbolism between 1889 and 1892 supported him in many of the ideas he had already formed, his reading of Friedrich Nietzsche gave a new authority to his poetic philosophy. He began to read Nietzsche seriously in the summer of 1902[36] and found that 'Nietzsche completes Blake and has the same roots';[37] he was fascinated by Nietzsche, and called him a 'strong enchanter'.[38] The Nietzschean element in *The King's Threshold* is apparent from the beginning in the versions of 1904 and 1906, and is further emphasized in the revised ending of 1922.

Where There is Nothing, published in November, 1902, shows Yeats under Nietzsche's spell. Zarathustra's exhortation to man to laugh helped to shape the hero, Paul Ruttledge, who declares:

My wild beast is laughter, the mightiest of the enemies of God.[39]

The idea of the regeneration of man, which Yeats found symbolized by Blake in the 'New Jerusalem', is proclaimed by Nietzsche in the coming birth of the 'superman'. Although Yeats never believed in the philosophy of the 'superman', *The King's Threshold* refers to 'the great race that is to come' resembling a race of 'supermen', who enjoy the Nietzschean gift of laughter:

> The stars had come so near me that I caught
> Their singing. It was praise of that great race
> That would be haughty, mirthful, and white-bodied,
> With a high head, and open hand, and how,
> Laughing, it would take the mastery of the world.

> (p. 135)

In the Nietzschean conception laughter announces the advent of the superman. Moreover, laughter is associated earlier in the play with the idea of destruction, when Seanchan explains the nature of poetry:

---

[36] *The letters of W.B. Yeats*, p. 379, Letter to Lady Gregory.
[37] Ibid.
[38] Ibid.
[39] W.B. Yeats, *Plays for an Irish Theatre* (Vol. i) (London, Bullen, 1911), p. 46.

> And I would have all know that when all falls
> In ruin, poetry calls out in joy,
> Being the scattering hand, the bursting pod,
> The victim's joy among the holy flame,
> God's laughter at the shattering of the world.
> And now that joy laughs out, and weeps and burns
> On these bare steps.

(p. 114)

Poetry is 'God's laughter at the shattering of the world', a vision which foreshadows the brazen winged beast associated with laughing ecstatic destruction in Yeats's poem 'The Second Coming', and the tragic gaiety of 'Lapis Lazuli'. In the latter, the three Chinamen look down upon the destruction and smile:

> On all the tragic scene they stare.
> One asks for mournful melodies;
> Accomplished fingers begin to play.
> Their eyes mid many wrinkles, their eyes,
> Their ancient, glittering eyes, are gay.[40]

There is also in *The King's Threshold* an emphasis on joy—a laughing joy. Seanchan expresses the joy of life in more than one passage: he calls marriage 'the height of life', and a little earlier he speaks sensuously of 'the ruddy flesh and the thin flanks/And the broad shoulders worthy of desire'. This connection between laughter and destruction may be explained by the fact that great and beautiful creations can be achieved only through sacrifice. Every new birth is a form of destruction as well as of creation:

> All things fall and are built again,
> And those that build them again are gay.[41]

This is why the joy of poetic creation depends partly on destruction; for thus it asserts its own indestructibility, and its endless fertility:

> Cry aloud
> That when we are driven out we come again
> Like a great wind that runs out of the waste
> To blow the tables flat.

(p. 128)

[40] Yeats, *Collected Poems*, p. 339.   [41] Ibid.

As Miss Ellis-Fermor explains:

> This is the apocalyptic vision of the function of poetry; through
> poetry, something breaks in upon life, bringing with it a terrible
> illumination from the world behind the world, so that the im-
> manent spirit passes suddenly from the unseen to the seen, from
> hidden to manifest; there can be no compromise between it and
> the world, for what it declares is the 'Word' and it is 'The Prophet
> of the Most High God'.[42]

This 'apocalyptic vision of the function of poetry' brings about a
regeneration of the intellect and the spirit. The survival of poetry and
the values it generates is ensured by means of a spiritual inheritance:

> O more than kin, O more than children could be,
> For children are but born out of our blood
> And share our frailty. O my chicks, my chicks!
> That I have nourished underneath my wings
> And fed upon my soul.
>
> (p. 141)

The three ideas, of great art, of aristocratic tradition, and of spiritual
inheritance, which grow more closely associated as time goes on, are
first combined in this play.

V

Although *The King's Threshold* is a relatively early expression
of Yeats's poetic faith it made possible his later magnificent pronouncements on the theory of poetry as he understood it. The poet
had projected one of his own crises in the crisis he created for
Seanchan. The process by which he overcame this crisis of belief is
expressed in the play, in the idea that, to achieve artistic perfection,
the artist must pledge himself unreservedly to poetry. In *The King's
Threshold* Seanchan makes an heroic stand for the ideal of poetry
which, as we have seen, is no less than 'the greatest of Divine
Revelations' and demanded the total allegiance of the poet even to
the extent of martyrdom. In identifying art with life Yeats makes
Seanchan carry out the full implication of the equation by suffering
martyrdom for the rights of poetry. Thus the poet rises to heroic
stature, in fact, by sacrificing himself for the supreme value of his art.

Yeats believed that if a man was prepared to live for an ideal or a
faith, he should equally be prepared to die for it. This is exactly what

[42] Ellis-Fermor, *The Irish Dramatic Movement*, p. 94.

distinguishes a great man from a small one, and this, indeed, is the greatest distinction of Yeats's tragic hero. All his heroes are prepared to live dangerously, yet heroically.

The King's Threshold is therefore both a dramatization of Yeats's theory of poetry and his vision of the poet as hero. It marks the point at which his poetic faith abandoned passivity for an active fight and descended from the realms on high to the world of reality. For if Forgael in *The Shadowy Waters* can be said to represent the poet or artist in isolation, preoccupied with his own dreams that make him an ineffectual seer moving on the edge of the real world, Seanchan, on the other hand, represents the poet or artist as man of action, resolved to become part of the real world and prepared to struggle with the trivialities of life to assert his position. In so doing, Yeats adopts the mask which was the fullest expression of his image of himself. For I think we have seen enough from Yeats's arguments in defence of poetry, thus far, to make a very close association between Seanchan, the Irish bard, and Yeats's own conception of himself as bard and hero-figure in one.

Yeats was constantly animated by the ideals he expressed in *The King's Threshold*. It reflects, in Seanchan's heroic stand, Yeats's own struggle for Ireland's intellectual freedom, and his belief in the primacy of the artist's function and role in society. Yeats is demanding in this play that he be given the selfsame rights that Seanchan demands. The rights of poetry were as true for modern as for ancient Ireland. Throughout his life, Yeats made the same stand on their behalf as Seanchan does in the play. Seanchan's stand is actually an heroic passivity, showing that sometimes the greatest heroism is necessarily manifested in inaction. This requires the greater moral courage and vision which I stressed earlier. Such a heroism, far from being anachronistic, remains pre-eminently true for all times in its appeal to human courage and vision. It might be called superhuman, in that it sets itself the highest standard, alone without succour. If the hero be required to stand alone in this, like Seanchan, he will readily do so. For, as we have seen, the province of poetry is eternal and looks forward to future generations and a better race of men which it will form:

> But I am labouring
> For some that shall be born in the nick o'time,
> And find sweet nurture, that they may have voices,
> Even in anger, like the strings of harps.   (p. 113)

The same basic qualities and ideals as Seanchan's are seen in Yeats's other great hero from Irish Myth, Cuchulain. Indeed of all the masks which Yeats adopted, Cuchulain most appealed to Yeats's 'need for self-dramatization', and he affords the closest parallel to Seanchan, as he appears in *On Baile's Strand*. In contrast to the poet's heroic passivity, Cuchulain displays the active poetic values in his spontaneity and imagination:

> I'll not be bound.
> I'll dance or hunt, or quarrel or make love,
> Wherever and whenever I've a mind to.[43]

Although Seanchan upholds the Court, whereas Cuchulain is unrestrained and sanguinary, they are united in their spontaneity. For Cuchulain draws his inspiration from the poet in the first place:

> Cry out that not a man alive
> Would ride among the arrows with high heart,
> Or scatter with an open hand, had not
> Our heady craft commended wasteful virtues.
>
> (p. 127)

Both King Guaire in *The King's Threshold* and Conchubor in *On Baile's Strand*, in comparison, stand for order and expediency. Their respective arguments with Seanchan and Cuchulain centre on the pair's disqualification to have a voice in matters of government. Cuchulain actually does not wish this anyway for he is too busy fighting to pay heed to Conchubor's reproof that he has neglected Aoife's threat to the realm. Wishing to placate his warrior tributary, for unlike the poet Cuchulain wields effective power, Conchubor proposes a parity between his wisdom and Cuchulain's strength; but, in demanding an oath, Conchubor really means to subordinate Cuchulain. Seanchan, in contrast, has his ancient right as poet to sit at the council table simply taken away:

> It was the men who ruled the world,
> And not the men who sang it, who should sit
> Where there was the most honour.
>
> (p. 109)

---

[43] Yeats, *Collected Plays*, p. 255.

Yet the opposition to both heroes is at heart directed against their threat to a staid order. Seanchan's is through his power as poet:

> But I that sit a throne,
> And take my measure from the needs of State,
> Call his wild thought that overruns the measure,
> Making words more than deeds, and his proud will
> That would unsettle all, most mischievous
> And he himself a most mischievous man.

(p. 110)

The King sent his messengers to buy off Seanchan. 'His wild thought that overruns the measure' is of the same stuff as Cuchulain's uncontrollable instinct to fight and make love, and he can no more be bought off than can the warrior, of whom Conchubor's children complain:

> How can we be at safety with this man
> That nobody can buy or bid or bind?
>
> He burns the earth as if he were a fire,
> And time can never touch him.[44]

Cuchulain is the legendary warrior-hero who represents all 'the wasteful virtues', and Seanchan is the poet whose 'heady craft commended' them.

Other Yeatsian heroes show similar vision and spontaneity to Seanchan's and Cuchulain's. Major Robert Gregory, for example, is moved to be an airman for no other reason than personal bravery and the exultation of flying:

> Nor law, nor duty bade me fight,
> Nor public men, nor cheering crowds,
> A lonely impulse of delight
> Drove to this tumult in the clouds.[45]

Similarly, his horsemanship defied prosaic concern for safety:

> At Mooneen he had leaped a place
> So perilous that half the astonished meet
> Had shut their eyes . . .[46]

[44] Ibid., pp. 255–6.
[45] Yeats, *Collected Poems,* p. 152.   [46] Ibid., p. 150.

Of the poets Yeats had known, Dowson and Johnson were singled out as heroes for their defiance of mercenary calculation and respect for their art. Though they met their ends in some dissipation, they kept the 'Muses' sterner laws':

> You had to face your ends when young—
> 'Twas wine or women, or some curse—
> But never made a poorer song
> That you might have a heavier purse,
> Nor gave loud service to a cause
> That you might have a troop of friends.
> You kept the Muses' sterner laws,
> And unrepenting faced your ends,
> And therefore earned the right—and yet
> Dowson and Johnson most I praise—
> To troop with those the world's forgot,
> And copy their proud steady gaze.[47]

Then there were the two martyrs, John Synge the poet and Terence MacSwiney the patriot. Both possessed the same heroic nature for Yeats, and both had a bearing upon *The King's Threshold*. For both Synge's death, which Yeats considered the greatest sacrifice yet made for Ireland's intellectual glory, and MacSwiney's sacrifice for Ireland's national integrity, seem to have inspired Yeats to revise the ending of his play. MacSwiney's death occurred in 1920 as a result of a hunger-strike in protest against his political imprisonment by the British. His fast lasted for seventy-three days, and no sooner had the circumstances of his death become known in Ireland than he was acclaimed a hero, a Nationalist martyr, and saint. Yeats was silent about the affair, but was evidently deeply moved and his feelings probably accorded fully with those expressed by Lady Gregory:

> For by his death and endurance he has made it unnecessary for any other prisoners to protest through hunger-strike; he has done it once for all.[48]

Seanchan's struggle has become a reality, and was now part of Ireland's history and heritage.

[47] Ibid., pp. 116–17.
[48] *Lady Gregory's Journal: 1916–1930*, edited by Lennox Robinson (Dublin, Putnam and Co. Ltd, 1946), p. 64.

No less formative was the example of Synge, a personal friend whom Yeats not only admired highly as an artist, but who was instrumental in changing Yeats's own approach to art. Synge's thought seems to have enabled Yeats to appreciate for the first time the 'delight in setting the hard virtues by the soft, the bitter by the sweet, salt by mercury, the stone by the elixir'.[49] He came to admire Synge's 'hunger for harsh facts, for ugly surprising things, for all that defies our hopes'.[50] This aspect of Synge's thought led Yeats to develop in himself an appetite for the 'savage imagination' as a whole. He also adopted Synge's example in using extreme types of human personality—the Fool and the Blind Man, in *On Baile's Strand*, and the Cripples, in *The King's Threshold*, are early examples. Synge also influenced Yeats in such matters as humour, and in his non-didactic approach to art strengthened Yeats's own.

Synge's death in 1909, at thirty-seven, was a bitter event for Yeats. Living, he 'was proud and lonely', almost self-sufficient in his genius; dying, he was transformed into a hero, a martyr of literature. Yeats would never forgive Ireland for its persecution of the man in whom he saw 'a great writer, the beginning it may be of a European figure'.[51] His belief that Synge's life had been shortened is evident in his Journal:

> I went to see Synge yesterday and found him ill: if he dies it will set me wondering if he could have lived had he not had his long misunderstanding with the wreckage of Young Ireland. Even a successful performance of one of his plays seems to have made him ill.[52]

Synge's death also symbolized Seanchan's struggle, though on a different level and in different circumstances from MacSwiney's.

Seanchan's triumph is moral and spiritual. His victory lies in the fact that he could achieve what none of those that surrounded him could: self-fulfilment through an heroic gesture, more effective and lasting than the whole arsenal of the King's armies. He has dared to live dangerously, yet heroically. To such a man—as for any of Yeats's

---

[49] Yeats, *Essays and Introductions*, p. 308.
[50] Ibid.
[51] Quoted by D.H. Greene and E.M. Stephens, *J.M. Synge: 1871–1909* (New York, Macmillan, 1959), p. 270. Unpublished Letter to Horace Plunkett, 1904.
[52] W.B. Yeats, *Autobiographies* (London, Macmillan, 1966), pp. 472–3.

heroes aforementioned—death meant 'glad tidings', because it was the manner in which a man lived and died that really mattered. The spiritual station of the soul that goes to take its abode amongst 'the high waters and mountain birds' depended on how worthy that soul proved itself 'to claim a portion of their solitude'. That is why the words 'Dead faces laugh' do not imply any contradiction; death has brought Seanchan utmost joy. This laughter is the material expression of tragic joy. Perhaps we could say of Seanchan's death what Lady Gregory said of MacSwiney's: 'he has done it once for all.'

VI

It is then for its fusion of heroic ideal and the vindication of the power of poets that The King's Threshold stands as one of Yeats's most impressive works. Universal in its appeal, it makes a comment on the archetypal significance of poetry which remains as relevant now as ever. It includes Yeats's complete conception of the artist's function and his place in society, as well as embodying many of his intimate convictions about poetry, art, life, aristocracy, tradition, love, and heroic achievement. It explains where his loyalties lay as far as Ireland and Art were concerned, and it presents his demands on his nation and the world, as a man of genius speaking on behalf of other men of genius.

Notes on contributors

Robert Burchfield is Chief Editor of the Oxford English Dictionaries and a past President of the English Association. Until 1979 he was a Fellow and Tutor in English Language at St Peter's College, Oxford. His best-known work is the *Supplement to the Oxford English Dictionary*, Volume I A–G (1972), Volume 2 H–N (1976), and Volume 3 O–Scz (1982).

John Pitcher is a Fellow and Tutor in English at St John's College, Oxford. He is editing the poems and plays of Samuel Daniel for the Oxford University Press. His first book, *Samuel Daniel: The Brotherton Manuscript: A Study in Authorship*, was published in 1981. He is writing a study of Jacobean women.

Bernard Sharratt has been Lecturer in English and American Literature, University of Kent at Canterbury, since 1971. He has published essays in various periodicals and collections, and is the author of *Reading Relations: structures of literary production: a dialectical textbook*, forthcoming from Harvester Press.

Claude Rawson is Professor of English at the University of Warwick. His books include *Henry Fielding and the Augustan Ideal Under Stress* and *Gulliver and the Gentle Reader*. He is an editor of the *Modern Language Review* and the *Yearbook of English Studies* and General Editor of the Unwin Critical Library. He is a Past President of the British Society for Eighteenth-Century Studies.

Kathleen Raine is an authority on the Neoplatonic and other sources of William Blake, and of other English Romantic poets, including W.B. Yeats. On Blake she has published a number of books, of which her latest, *The Human Face of God* (on the illustrations of the Book of Job), will appear early in 1982, as also will her collected papers on W.B. Yeats. She is also a critic, autobiographer and poet.

Alastair Thomson is Professor of English at the New University of Ulster. His publications include *Valéry* (1965), and an anthology of critical essays on Wordsworth, *Wordsworth's Mind and Art* (1969).

Suheil Badi Bushrui is Professor of English and Anglo-Irish Literature at the American University of Beirut, Lebanon. A Ph.D. of Southampton University, he has taught and lectured in many countries. Besides two volumes of his own Arabic poetry, he has written on English, Arabic, and African literatures. His four books on W.B. Yeats include the first full-length critical study in Arabic. He is also an authority on Kahlil Gibran. He holds the Presidency of the Association of University Teachers of English in the Arab World.